A BRIEF HISTORY OF THE PRESENT

'In this book, Hilal Ahmed analyses the relationship of Hindutva with its various facets—historical, cultural, social and political—of Muslim life in a "New India". We learn a lot about the inner diversity of Muslim society, the complexities of Pasmanda politics, the absence of affection for Aurangzeb among India's Muslims, the weakness of Muslim liberals to strike roots in the Muslim community and much more. Enlightening!'
—**Ashutosh Varshney, director, Saxena Center for Contemporary South Asia, Sol Goldman Professor of International Studies and the Social Sciences and Professor of Political Science at Watson Institute for International and Public Affairs, Brown University**

'It's a measure of Hilal Ahmed's optimism in India's ability to self-heal that he draws lessons for the future from the past. Measured and restrained, *A Brief History of the Present* steers clear of emotionalism, preferring pragmatic reflection to put the state of Indian Muslims in context, and using that context to shine a light to the way ahead. Suffused with hope, Ahmed's latest offering treads the middle path. No mean feat in these times of extremities'
—**Ghazala Wahab, editor, FORCE, and author of *Born a Muslim: Some Truths about Islam in India* (winner of the Book of the Year Award [non-fiction] Tata Literature Live 2021 and Atta Galatta-Bangalore Literature Festival Book of the Year 2021 [non-fiction])**

'In this provocative new book, Hilal Ahmed skilfully examines the place of Muslims in the "New India". Building on a career's worth of qualitative and quantitative research, he asks and answers uncomfortable questions about "Muslimness" in an era of Hindu nationalist hegemony. The book challenges popular arguments touted by both liberals and conservatives'
—**Milan Vaishnav, director and senior fellow, South Asia Program, Carnegie Endowment for International Peace**

A BRIEF HISTORY OF THE PRESENT

Muslims in New India

HILAL AHMED

PENGUIN
VIKING
An imprint of Penguin Random House

VIKING

Viking is an imprint of the Penguin Random House group of companies
whose addresses can be found at global.penguinrandomhouse.com

Published by Penguin Random House India Pvt. Ltd
4th Floor, Capital Tower 1, MG Road,
Gurugram 122 002, Haryana, India

Penguin
Random House
India

First published in Viking by Penguin Random House India 2024

Copyright © Hilal Ahmed 2024

10 9 8 7 6 5 4 3 2 1

ISBN 9780670094356

Typeset in Adobe Caslon Pro by MAP Systems, Bengaluru, India
Printed at Replika Press Pvt. Ltd, India

www.penguin.co.in

Nazima Parveen,
. . . life partner and intellectual comrade!

Contents

Introduction

I

Personal is political!

On 31 July 2023, in an incident widely reported in the press, a Railway Protection Force (RPF) constable allegedly killed four innocent people—his senior officer, Tikaram Meena and three passengers. All of them were travelling in the Jaipur–Mumbai Central Superfast Express. The three passengers were identified as Abdul Qadirbhai Mohammed Hussain Bhanpurwala, Akhtar Abbas Ali and Sadar Mohammed Hussain.[1] According to media reports, the accused constable was heard saying, *'Pakistan se operate hue ye, aur media yehi coverage dikha rahi hai, unko sab pata chal raha hai ye kya kar rahe hain . . . Agar vote dena hai, agar Hindustan mein rehna hai to mai kehta hoon Modi aur Yogi, ye do hain* [They are being operated from Pakistan, our media is also showing this, they know what they are doing . . . I say if they want to live in Hindustan and if they want to vote . . . Modi and Yogi are the only option].'[2]

This was a highly disturbing event. It underlined the fact that anti-Muslim discourse in India has reached an extremely violent level. The established markers of Muslim presence—skull cap, beard, Hijab, minarets of mosques and even an advertisement written in Urdu—are being perceived as civilizational threats to Hinduism. Muslims are targeted, abused, insulted and even lynched to death in public to assert nationalism in overtly Hindu terms.[3] It does not stop here. A section of the media further contributes to this hostile anti-Muslim environment. An impression is created that Muslims are responsible for every problem in the country. They are untrustworthy; their loyalty to the nation is questionable; they are highly organized; they are involved in conspiracies against India/Hindus; and their religion permits them to get involved in anti-India propaganda. These are just a few accusations attached to them. A leading news anchor, in fact, prepared a flowchart to explain the nature of jihad in India.[4]

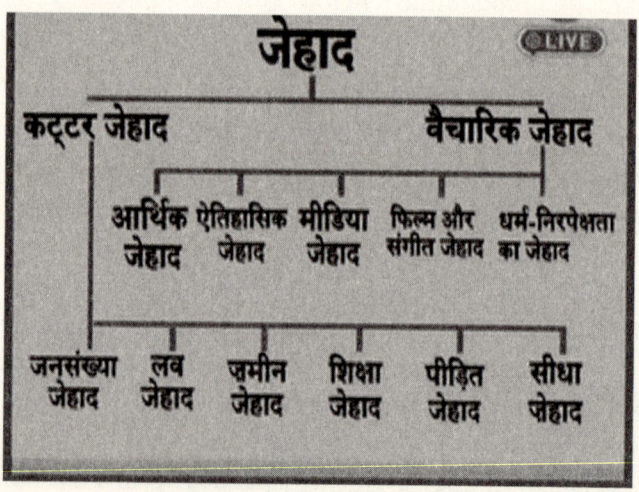

Figure 1: Jihad flowchart!
Source: (Newslaundry)[5]

(Translation: The flowchart identifies two main types of jihads: fundamentalist and intellectualist. Fundamentalist jihad is then subdivided into population jihad, love jihad, land jihad, education jihad, charity jihad and 'plain' jihad. Intellectualist jihad is subdivided into financial jihad, historical jihad, media jihad, films and music jihad and secularist jihad.)

This aggressive anti-Muslim environment upsets me deeply. It goes against the two principles I have always cherished: my spiritual faith in Almighty Allah and my belief in the Gandhian ideal of 'sarva dharma sambhav [all religions can co-exist]'.[6] I find it hard to think only as a 'Muslim' as if this is the only identity attribute I have. I follow a liberative interpretation of Islam that encourages me to offer namaz and observe fast without giving up my commitment to the larger issues of social justice and economic equality. In this sense, I am more than a Muslim.

This 'more than Muslim' identity, however, goes against the established political correctness. Hindutva politics categorizes Muslims as a monolithic religious group to substantiate Hindu homogeneity. The liberals, on the other hand, claim to protect Muslims as a religious minority to defend Indian democracy (if not secularism!). In both cases, Muslim identity is envisioned as a one-dimensional phenomenon.

The outcome is obvious. In the last five years, I have been politely advised by well-meaning acquaintances to change the topic of my lectures and talks simply to deal with the 'pressure from outside'. My discourse on topics such as 'Muslim Politics in India', 'Rethinking Minorities' and even the 'Nation and its (Unwanted) Fragments' have made the organizers uncomfortable. In fact, a few such events were eventually cancelled. At the same time, I am also asked by a vocal section of netizens to be thankful to Hindus that they have tolerated me in India. According to these X (formerly Twitter) nationalists, I survive on 'taxpayers' money'.

What went wrong?

I belong to a generation that grew up in the 1990s. That is when the many versions of today's India began to take shape— including Hindutva India and the politics of social justice and

xiv   Introduction

equity. We forcefully rejected the Hindu-Muslim divide, histories of Partition, the dominance of the English-speaking urban elite, caste-based prejudices, patriarchal values and gender injustice. We forged a new set of values without being apologetic about our religious/caste identities and our class locations.

This moral–political imagination of the 1990s was different from the nation-building project of Nehruvian elites. There was a *radical* impulse in it—a commitment to create a just and egalitarian society. In this creative-radical context, it was possible to think of a liberative, pro-people and *secular* interpretation of Islam and Hinduism. Something that progressive religious thinkers and activists like Asghar Ali Engineer and Swami Agnivesh conceptualized and practised.

This political imagination, however, suffered from two internal problems. It paid no attention to the idea of comprehensive socio–political transformation and reduced the radical impulse to electoral calculations. The so-called coalition of Dalit–Muslims–Backward was nothing but an electoral game plan used and nurtured by the political elite.

The moral decline of political parties and the subsequent transformation of many people's movements into funded NGOs, paved the way for a strange political correctness, an imagination of a fragile secular network of 'progressive' and 'deprived' sections—Muslims, Dalits, women, Adivasis, workers, peasants, displaced communities, people with disabilities and so on.

This conception had an internal contradiction. These segments of society were seen as inherently progressive and secular. This assumption was so strong that there was virtually no discussion on the composition of this progressive-secular camp and its power elite. There was a fear that critical questioning might disturb the equilibrium of this network and would strengthen what was then called the 'communal-regressive forces'.[7]

There was a second problem as well. This tendency to view some sections as inherently progressive meant that the rest were adversaries. That meant viewing the 'north Indian-Hindi-speaking-upper-caste-religiously-practising-Hindu-male' as responsible for social backwardness, institutional exclusions and communal prejudices against others.

It was a fertile ground for Hindutva politics. It became easier for the Hindutva groups to raise the question of nationalism as well as the marginalization of Hindu religious identity in the public sphere.[8] In this volatile political context, something else happened—Muslims were given the status of a recognized, permanent national minority under the National Commission for Minorities Act 1993. In a way, this officially transformed Hindus into a national religious majority for the first time in independent India.[9] The outcome of these processes became evident in post-2014 India when that older 1990s discourse of inclusion was replaced by a powerful assertion of Hindu victimhood.[10] This is what I have tried to do in this book—discuss this process and its outcomes.

II

Political correctness and public debates

For an intellectual who is not dependent on income generated by clickbait articles, what explains the need to write so frequently? If you want to pose as a public intellectual you need to clarify whose interests are being advocated and protected by your writing . . . If it's purely academic rumination then write well-researched and well-considered peer-reviewed articles in academic journals, not these dozens of articles every month.

I received this WhatsApp message from a well-meaning intellectual, who was a bit upset with me because I write 'unnecessarily nuanced and academic-oriented' articles in newspapers and web portals regularly. Obviously, this person is unaware of my 'academic writings'—in Hindi and English.

I do not want him/her to read my CV. Nor I am interested in defending my public writings. Yet, I am persuaded to respond to this ill-informed, unkind and completely reactionary comment because it is based on an assumption that public discussions are only meant for simple, straightforward and ready-to-use answers.

It reminds us that a dividing line is often created between 'nuanced-jargon-oriented academic' discourse and 'easy-to-understand' journalistic type of writing. This dividing line has been one of the main reasons behind the deteriorating level of intellectual engagement. A section of public commentators—those who frequently contribute to newspapers and web portals—remain indifferent towards serious academic works. This apathy makes their explanations shallow and superficial. The academics, on the other hand, fail to understand the significance of contemporary questions. They are always late in responding to social issues, which set the contours of our public life. Let me elaborate on this puzzle by highlighting three intrinsic problems of our public debates.

Three problems

There is a belief that the Constitution is a permanent reference point for determining the everyday business of our political life. This belief is not entirely incorrect. It is true that the Constitution has established certain normative ideals to provide guiding principles to the government. It does not, however, mean that the practicalities of politics are always determined by these principles. The political class interprets these principles as per its own requirements and produces their politically effective and applicable meanings.

For example, the Constitution was interpreted as a source to justify the state's intervention in the economic life of the country, immediately after the Independence. The 'public sector', 'planning' and 'socialistic pattern' were the keywords of our public discourse in the 1960s and 1970s. The Constitution was, however, interpreted in a completely different way after economic liberalization in early 1990s. The State now claims that the market is capable of regulating itself; hence, there is no need to intervene in the economic domain.[11]

Market-driven economic policies, in a way, have restructured political institutions in a radical manner in the last three decades. The establishment of Special Economic Zones (SEZs) and the introduction of Goods and Services Tax (GST) are not merely simple economic initiatives. They have far-reaching impacts on local-level institutions as well as federal relations. Our public debates, unfortunately, do not recognize such complex and direct interconnections between the economy and polity. Consequently, a rigid interpretation of political institutions continues to survive.

This brings us to another related problem. It is now fashionable to claim that there is no place for ideology in our politics. The Aam Aadmi Party (AAP) was instrumental in propagating this claim that ideology was a twentieth-century phenomenon that had no role to play in Indian politics.[12] It was also argued that 'good practices' would generate 'good ideas', which might form the basis for new political values and standards. In the post-ideological world, this formulation was deeply attractive, especially in the early 2010s. However, it had a very different practical implication.

Today, political parties no longer need to offer any ideological justification for electoral manoeuvrings and manipulations. They defend their practical moves in the name of winnability. Even the BJP, which proudly celebrates its association with the ideology of Hindutva, gives more importance to the winnability factor, especially when it comes to electoral politics.

Our public debates, interestingly, do not recognize the actual implications of this new form of politics. For instance, dominant sections of liberal intellectuals adhere to the view that Hindutva politics is simply a form of fascism in India. They are not interested in studying the changing positions of Sangh Parivar on the caste system, the internal contradictions/ debates among the Hindutva groups on economic liberalization, and even for that matter, on the Uniform Civil Code (UCC). This lack of engagement with changing political realities does not allow them to question their own assumptions and beliefs.

Finally, there is no space for serious future-oriented political imaginations in our public discourse. Political parties have already started behaving like 'political firms': they address voters as consumers; offer welfare packages to attract them; and treat the elections as a competitive market. This election-centric framework is built upon two conflicting impulses—the 'desirability of the package' for attracting a set of voters, and at the same time, the 'creation of an enemy', an 'Other', who could be projected as a threat. UPA's politics of secularism and inclusion, for instance, envisaged the inclusion of marginalized groups as a welfare package while projecting BJP's Hindutva as a threat to the nation. The BJP, interestingly, also follows a very similar logic. It talks of *labharthis* (welfare beneficiaries) to reach out to marginalized households. At the same time, Muslim identity is deliberately problematized to describe anti-BJP electoral politics as a form of 'minority appeasement'. It shows that political parties do not need to invest in the idea of comprehensive social transformation.

There is no such compulsion for the intellectual class. They can certainly go beyond the limits set by the political parties. No doubt that Gandhi, Ambedkar, Bhagat Singh, Lohia, Jayaprakash Narayan, Savarkar, Deen Dayal Upadhyaya, Maulana Azad and Nehru have been seriously discussed and criticized in public debates in recent years. This engagement with modern Indian political thought is very valuable.

However, these debaters also strangely over-rely on these figures. They are often evoked to discover answers to contemporary questions. This reductionist approach is deeply problematic. The great thinkers of the past can certainly be our reference points for making sense of our political realities. But we must discover other intellectual resources as well to explore our political universe in its entirety. The present study is an attempt to make a meaningful academic intervention to address these questions of our public life.

III

Framework: Hindutva, Muslimness and a history of the present

'History of the present' is perhaps a provocative title, especially when it is employed in relation to Muslims of India. It is a well-known fact that Islam is the second largest Indian religion, and Muslims constitute almost 14 per cent of the country's population.[13] This 'community of believers' is highly diversified—they are divided on caste, class, region and even sub-religious lines. To make any authoritative claim about 'the present' of India's Muslims, hence, is a challenging task. Yet I do want to take up this challenge for three very specific reasons.

First, I make a crucial distinction between 'substantive Muslimness' and 'discourse Muslimness'. Substantive Muslimness refers to the multiple ways in which Muslim identity is formed in a variety of regional and local contexts. Caste, language, class and region play a significant role in determining the self-perception of a Muslim individual in real-life situations.

Various survey-based studies conducted by the Centre for the Study of Developing Societies (CSDS)–Lokniti clearly show that Muslim perceptions, views, opinions and attitudes do not follow any set pattern.[14] We do not even find a homogeneous response to questions related to basic religious practices such as offering *Namaz* and observing fasts (Roza) in the month of

Ramzan. This Muslim diversity underlines the fact that Indian Islam as a lived religion is practised by Muslims in a variety of ways. This is what I call 'substantive Muslimness'.

The 'discourse of Muslimness', however, underlines a different aspect of Indian Muslim identity. Their classification as a religious minority in purely statistical terms, the description of medieval Indian history as Islamic rule and the media debates around Islamic jihad and terrorism produce a simple and undifferentiated image of a homogeneous Muslim community. Every aspect of Muslim life is seen through the prism of this discourse either to criticize them for being barbaric or to celebrate their culture as a symbol of a royal Islamic past.

The interplay between substantive Muslimness and the discourse of Muslimness determines the actual manifestations of modern Indian Muslim identity in our public life. Substantive Muslimness gives it concrete real-life meanings, while the discourse of Muslimness converts the Muslim identity into a national/global question. The title *History of the Present*, in my view, captures this interesting trajectory of Muslim identity formation, which this book tries to explore.

Now, the second reason—the famous sociologist and one of the leading experts on Indian Islam, Imtiaz Ahmad makes a very significant argument. He finds a strange tendency among the scholars, who work on India's Muslims. These researchers, Ahmad argues, prioritize historical facts and categories to analyse the issues faced by contemporary Muslim societies.[15] As a result, the everydayness of Muslims could not become an object of serious analysis. This criticism, interestingly, is also valid for political discussions and public debates. The 'present' of India's Muslims is always seen as a residue of their past; and precisely for this reason, we encounter highly contentious representations of Muslim rule, and for that matter, Muslim heritage.

The distinction between the 'past' and 'history' is relevant to elaborate Ahmad's criticism. The 'past' is a multifaceted phenomenon and modern 'history' is one of the possible modes by which it is articulated and expressed. Memories, tales and narratives are equally powerful techniques to explore the past. The given histories of Muslim presence in India are certainly an important aspect of Muslims' imaginations. However, their everydayness does not entirely depend on such histories. Thus, we must acknowledge the significance of the past in the everyday situation of Muslims; and at the same time, pay serious attention to their highly diversified social-cultural universe. In other words, we have to historicize the 'here and now' of Muslims of India for the sake of producing a 'history of their present'.[16]

The third reason is related to an important aspect of our public life—the triumph of Hindutva as the dominant political narrative. Any discussion about Muslims of contemporary India cannot become meaningful if Hindutva as a political-ideological force is not given adequate importance. However, the term Hindutva is often used freely. The BJP, and for that matter, the organizations that recognize Hindutva as a 'way of life', employ this term in a generic manner. Often, they tend to go beyond V.D. Savarkar's conceptualization, who coined this term.[17] Savarkar identifies a few characteristics of the Hindu nation in his book *Hindutva*. For him, a clearly marked geography, a common language, a common culture and a belief that India is a 'holy land' constitute Hindutva as an ideology.[18] Contemporary Hindu nationalism, which proudly uses the term 'Hindutva' to describe its political outlook, however, does not entirely adhere to Savarkar's definition. Instead of defining Hindutva, a section of politicians, journalists and social influencers use it as a self-explanatory historical truth.[19] This strategic move helps them to establish Savarkar as a political icon without specifying their own meanings of the term 'Hindutva'.

Interestingly, even a section of liberal commentators does not pay attention to this important fact. They tend to evoke a rather conventional term, 'Sangh Parivar', to describe contemporary Hindutva as a form of fascism. This reductionist approach does not allow them to analyse the ever-changing constitution of Hindutva as a political force, which has been accepted even by the non-BJP parties as a serious point of departure. The placing of Muslimness in this highly vague entity called Hindutva requires a serious engagement with contemporary political developments.[20] This is what makes the term 'history of the present' analytically meaningful.

IV

Questions, methods, sources

It is expected from a researcher to clarify his/her intellectual objectives, the choice of research method(s), the process of research and finally the nature of conclusions and arguments. These protocols are to be followed to avoid any possibility of sweeping generalization. In pursuant to these professional requirements, let me introduce readers to my research objectives. More specifically, I ask three sets of questions that relate to the wider socio-economic changes and nature of Indian democracy; those focusing on the multifaceted idea of Hindutva and its varied manifestations; and finally, some concerning Muslim socio-political perceptions and anxieties in today's India.

Socio-economic context and the political class:

1. Why do we need to go beyond the popular explanations of Hindutva? Is there any relationship between the structural changes introduced by the political class in the last three decades and the growing anti-Muslim discourse in recent years?

2. What are the implications of these changes for Indian democracy?

3. Is only the BJP/RSS responsible for the decline of secular politics? What has happened to the secularism of the so-called secular parties of the 1990s?

Making sense of the Hindutva vs liberal binary

4. What is the nature of Hindutva politics? What is the placing of Muslim presence in the Hindutva political discourse? How can we explain the BJP's inclination to mobilize Pasmanda Muslim communities?

5. What is the liberal position on contemporary politics? How does the non-BJP intelligentsia define Muslim identity? Who are liberal Muslims? How do they respond to Muslim anxieties?

6. What are 'Muslim issues'? How does a particular subject or an event become a 'Muslim issue'?

Muslim responses

7. Are all Muslims anti-BJP and anti-Modi? What are their perceptions and anxieties?

8. What has happened to Islam as a religion? Has Hindutva discourse forced Muslims to become more Islamic?

9. Have Muslims given up politics in India?

To explore the specific nature of these questions, the book relies on five kinds of sources.

Official documents, such as the parliamentary debates, Census reports and election reports published by the Election Commission of India, are the first kind of sources. These documents are used to extract relevant information/data to offer an informed, evidence-based narrative.

Published material (pamphlets, short books in various languages and rare photographs) which I have been collecting for over two decades during my fieldwork in different parts of India is the second major source of information. These ethnographic details provide 'thick background' descriptions to situate my main arguments.

I believe that speeches delivered by religious leaders and politicians provide relevant first-hand information on critical issues. These speeches also introduce us to different perspectives and positions. This is the reason why speeches are taken as an important source. The fourth kind of sources may be called the online sources. The websites of leading religious and political organizations, online newspaper reports and articles are very relevant for understanding the public perceptions and debates about contemporary Muslim politics.

The data generated by the CSDS–Lokniti on various aspects of Muslim social and political lives in post-1947 India is my fifth source. The National Election Study (NES) data sets have been used for offering a comparative analysis of Muslim politics. The 'Religious Attitudes and Behaviours Survey 2015' (which was designed primarily to make sense of the contemporary forms of religiosity in India), and the findings of my two ongoing research projects on 'Muslim Leadership in India' and 'Religious and Political Attitudes of Muslim Communities' (based on 'Religion in India: Tolerance and Segregation' conducted by the Pew Research Center) are also be used extensively to understand the complex making of the Muslim political identity.[21]

I use survey data as empirical evidence to understand the nature of issues such as political anxieties, religiosity and imaginations of the past. This methodological preference raises an important question. Religion, especially when it is understood as a form of spirituality, is often described as a philosophical phenomenon—an experience that is easy to feel but difficult to explain. The quantification of religiosity, we are told, is problematic if not entirely undesirable. I do recognize the main thrust of this critique. Yet, I am not fully convinced that this line of reasoning is analytically helpful, especially in the Indian context. The spiritual-philosophical aspects of religion become more apparent when they are translated into actual social practices.[22] It is, therefore, analytically legitimate to measure Muslim self-perceptions through the survey method. It does not, however, mean that quantitative data and empirical details are self-explanatory hard facts. In my view, survey data does not provide any fixed, clear-cut and unmistakable answers to the complex real-life questions. Instead, the quantitative data comes to us as 'raw information' that would become meaningful and explanatory if it is placed in a fully worked-out theoretical framework.

V

What I do and what I do not do

The structure of the book aims to provide a sequence to our identified research questions. Following the Introduction, there are eight main chapters. I explore the question of 'more than a Muslim identity' in Chapter 1. This chapter attempts to explore the relationship between academic/intellectual work and the political positioning of a Muslim researcher in contemporary India. I raise a few conceptual problems and methodological questions, especially in relation to my intellectual engagement with Muslim communities. Through these questions, I discuss those methodological issues that I encounter while working on various facets of Muslim political identity. Chapter 2 explores the idea of New India in its entirety. It pays close attention to the political-structural changes introduced by the BJP regime after 2014. These changes are studied in relation to the postcolonial legal-constitutional discourse to find out the official meanings of a few important themes like 'India as the mother of democracy', 'New India' and *Sabka Saath, Sabka Vikas, Sabka Vishwas*. I try to make sense of these themes to understand the changing nature of the State in India. I describe this phenomenon as the 'Chartable State'. Chapter 3 discusses the various ways in which the Muslim past is reconfigured in New India. It touches upon the 'Hinduism versus Hindutva' debate to find out the constitution of the Muslim 'historical' in recent years. Chapter 4 discusses this further by looking into the nature of contemporary political debates related to Muslim heritage. This chapter examines the Gyanvapi mosque controversy and the figure of Aurangzeb to map out the presentation of the cultural sphere of Muslims in New India. Chapter 5 is based on my ongoing work on contemporary Indian Islamic religiosity. This chapter shows the changing Muslim imaginations of Islam in New India. It is argued that Islamic religiosity is not always governed by the logic of Hindutva politics. Chapter 6 discusses the phenomenon called 'liberal Muslims'. Questioning the outdated and rigid interpretation of modernity, I try to underline the elitist nature of liberal Muslim discourse. I also show why the BJP is more interested in the 'right-kind of Muslims' rather than the liberals. Chapter 7 expands the scope of this discussion by investigating the 'Pasmanda question' and its political implications, especially in north India. A systematic explanation of caste–*biradari* formation among Muslims is offered to make sense of the BJP's Pasmanda politics. Finally, Chapter 8 examines the question of Muslim political participation. Evoking two meanings of political participation—'participation as interaction' and 'participation as instrumental action'—the chapter analyses the nature of Muslim politics in New India. The concluding chapter provides an analytical overview of the study by making a few explanatory arguments.

Let me make three clarifications to explain the scope of this book. I must confess that the book is focused on northern India. I do not claim to offer any analytically specific explanation of Muslim politics in the southern states. Yet, I am confident that my analytical framework is certainly useful in making sense of the ways in which Muslim identity and politics are intertwined at the state level. This modest claim is based on two premises. First, the contours of Muslim political discourse are always determined by north Indian political developments. The idioms, metaphors and even the vocabulary of politics used in the northern states are often transplanted at the state level. The love jihad and hijab issues are two crucial exceptions in this regard. Secondly, this book is interested in the big picture. Its purpose is to situate Muslimness as a political entity in the larger political–cultural and economic context. In this sense, it is not merely a study of Muslims in India; instead, I take Muslimness as a vantage point to make sense of the multifaceted idea of Indian democracy.[23] Finally, there is no 'ready-to-use political recipe' for the future. The book does not offer or even claim to offer any political advice to any community or political party/ coalition. It is an intellectual exercise, which aims to analyse political trends and attitudes.

Chapter 1

Muslimness and Intellectual Politics

I

Shall I speak as a Muslim?

The protests against the Citizenship (Amendment) Act (CAA), 2019—a law passed by the Indian Parliament that offers citizenship to non-Muslim religious communities of three Muslim majority states, namely Pakistan, Bangladesh and Afghanistan—is an important point of reference for this discussion.[1] A section of protestors argues, in fact quite stridently, that Muslims (including scholars and academics with Muslim names) should come forward and reclaim their Muslim identity as an 'affected minority'. Journalist Irena Akbar, for instance, writes:

> If Muslims are asserting their religious identity with their religious slogans, it is because they have been targeted on account of their religion. If the state wants to bully me because of my faith, I will only publicly assert it. Hannah Arendt, the Jewish political philosopher who fled Nazi Germany in the 1930s, wrote, 'If one is attacked as a Jew, one must defend oneself as a Jew. Not as a German, not as a world-citizen, not as an upholder of the Rights of Man.' A democracy allows

you to protest from your standpoint. An unaffected majority
can protest solely as an Indian. An affected minority has the
right to protest as an Indian and as a minority.[2]

Arguments of this kind led to a short-lived-yet-highly
controversial debate. It began in January 2020 when the anti-
CAA protests were going on throughout the country and
Delhi's Shaheen Bagh had emerged as the epicentre of this
new politics of resistance. A prominent BJP leader shared
a video clip of a speech delivered by a JNU student Sharjeel
Imam.[3] The police took swift action and Imam was arrested
under the Unlawful Activities (Prevention) Act. The media
described him as the mastermind of the anti-CAA protests.
The *Organizer,* the mouthpiece of the Rashtriya Swayamsewak
Sangh (RSS), published a detailed cover story on what it called
the 'separatist' anti-national politics of Imam in its February
2020 print edition.[4]

Anti-CAA protestors were somehow confused about this
question. There were two conflicting responses. The organizers
of the Shaheen Bagh protest took a very clear position. In order
to provide an inclusive character to the anti-CAA protests, the
Shaheen Bagh Committee issued a statement asserting that
'no one individual's videos, statements or articles can represent
the movement'.[5] On the other hand, a section of protestors
supported Imam's freedom of expression. Some of them, in fact,
recognized him as the 'voice of young Indian Muslims'.[6]

I was not in India and did not have sufficient information
to make any substantive comment or argument on this episode.
Nevertheless, I gave an interview to the television network,
NDTV, underlining the nature of BJP's CAA politics and
its keenness to appropriate the figure of Sharjeel Imam for
transforming the anti-CAA protest into a Hindu–Muslim
conflict. I also made it clear that although I was not fully aware

of the contents of Imam's controversial speech, I found his views objectionable and counterproductive. This minor comment was taken very seriously by pro-Imam intellectuals and activists.[7]

I was criticized for being a passive, inactive, self-contented, armchair liberal–secular intellectual, who would not dare to speak as a 'Muslim'. My professional affiliations were also invoked to describe me as an intellectual elite, who would intentionally make an unclear, tentative, less-political critique of the CAA in the name of 'nuanced' analysis.

This type of criticism is deeply rooted in the cultural universe of Indian academic and public lives. However, I do not underestimate two serious intellectual questions that emerge from these criticisms: how should I manage my professional identity as a researcher? And how should I deal with my deep cultural–philosophical associations with the version of Islam I recognize as my religion?

Let me elaborate on these puzzling issues. Muslimness of an individual or of a group as a 'lived experience' and the Muslim identity of a social/cultural group as an 'object of analysis' introduces us to two very different formulations. A Muslim, who lives in India, may accommodate various social, cultural, linguistic and even religious affiliations as lived experiences, without classifying them either as Indian or Islamic. However, when such lived experiences are transformed into 'objects' of analysis, the notion of identity or identities emerges as conceptual tools by which we try to make sense of the multifaceted cultural engagements and religious–ideological commitments of an individual or a group. Thus, many groups and communities, who live in different regions of India and in fact practice various forms of Islam, invariably become 'Indian Muslims'.

The legal–constitutional discourse in India, which recognizes Muslims as a religious minority, is another important source that provides a legal homogeneity to this pan-Indian identity of Muslims.[8] Indian Muslims are to be recognized not merely as individual citizens but also as members of a nationally recognized religious minority. This legal duality—secular citizenship versus minority rights as a religious community—has been one of the most contentious aspects of postcolonial Indian politics. Indian Muslims are often called a 'pampered community' and the minority rights given to them are described as a symbol of Muslim appeasement by the Hindu right-wing.[9]

It does not, however, mean that Muslim individual/groups, do not assert their collective Islamic identity. They prefer to describe themselves as Muslims in a variety of ways. These diverse expressions of Muslim-ness introduce us to the ever-changing collective self-perceptions of Muslim social group(s) and their imagined meanings of 'Islamic *ummah*' in the Indian context.[10] The Indian Muslim identity, in this sense, is not something that we merely discover through our research on concerned Muslim communities; rather, it has a cultural–sociological career of its own.

The Muslim identity of a researcher is another aspect of this 'Muslim identity' puzzle.[11] The Muslim identity of a researcher helps the researcher use his/her own experiences as a Muslim in forming the appropriate questions for respondents. S/he has access and are aware of the innermost characteristics and cultural nuances of the community.

However, the Muslim identity of a researcher has its limitations. Many a time, it becomes very difficult to draw a clear dividing line between the research questions and the cultural practices and affiliations, which one shares with the group/community. This becomes more complicated when Muslim researchers are asked to respond as some kind of representatives of the concerned Muslim community. In such cases, the professional ethics of research is somehow ignored and the thin dividing line between research and praxis is disregarded.

Thus, as a researcher on Muslim identity, I encounter three overlapping formulations:

a. As stated earlier, there is a difference between identities as lived experiences and identities as objects of analysis.

b. The objectivization of identities could have many forms. Thus, there is a difference between the 'constitution of identities in the public/political discourses' and the study of 'identities in academic discourses'.

c. The identity of a researcher is an important aspect, which should not be taken as 'given', especially, while doing social and political analysis.

II

Lived Islam: Faith as a researchable object

The distinction I make between identities as lived experiences and identities as objects of analysis underlines a productive tension between research exercise and everyday-ness.[12] In my view, we must take this distinction as a point of reference to understand the complex ways in which religious identity of an individual is formed. In my opinion, we do not think of resolving this tension; rather if we recognize it, we would be able to understand the discursive-ever-changing forms by which Islamic religiosities and imaginations of the collective past are constituted.[13] I would like to take two examples—changing mosque architecture and the language of Islam in postcolonial Delhi—to elaborate on this point.

The religious demography and sociological profile of Muslims of Delhi changed very rapidly in the 1990s. Economic liberalization, educational mobility and the migration of middle-class Muslims from neighbouring states played an important role in this regard. These changes also had a direct impact on the class configuration of Muslims. A new Muslim middle class has emerged, which is economically influential and religiously more practising. A section of this new middle class has embraced the Tablighi Jamaat—a religious reform movement that began in the in the late 1920s—as its preferred form of religiosity. The idea that Muslims should give up the ritualistic aspects of religion as well as this worldly consideration has been quite attractive for this class.[14] Since Tablighi Jamaat has always been a mosque-centric movement, it has become inevitable for this new middle class to redefine the mosque space.

In the last three decades, almost all the functional mosques in Delhi have been rebuilt quite extensively—not only in terms of size but also in terms of design and architectural features. The older forms of north Indian Sunni mosques, especially the local mosques, which were not built for large Friday congregational prayers, relied heavily on locally evolved architectural designs. That was the reason why the minaret was never treated as an essential or fundamental component of the mosque structure. A large number of mosques in the north Indian cities did not have a minaret at all. This trend has now changed. The minaret has found a new symbolic status in recent years. A considerable amount of money is spent to provide greater visibility to minarets.[15] In fact, there are ready-to-use minarets available in the market that can be installed to mark the symbolic presence of a mosque.

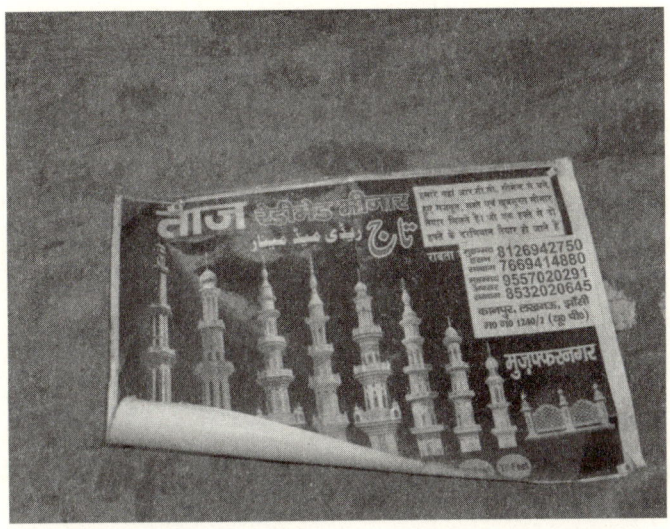

Figure 1.1: An advertisement for readymade minarets.

(Source: Author)

The design and architectural features are the most interesting aspects of these new minarets. One finds that Middle Eastern Islamic architectural symbols are preferred over the conventional Indo–Islamic architectural forms of minarets and domes (Figure 1.1).

The most significant change is the increasing use of Hindi in the religious discourses. This trend goes against the conventional view that Urdu has a deep connection with Islamic identity formation, especially in north India. The Muslim middle classes are employing Hindi for mass religious mobilization. Notice boards in mosques, signposts and even epitaphs in Muslim graveyards are now being written in the Devanagari script. One can find the Hindi versions of the Quran and Tablighi Jamaat's text *Fazae-le Amal* in almost every mosque in Delhi. In fact, the Hindi translations of all the known commentaries of the Quran written by Indian Ulama (religious scholars) are easily available.[16]

Figure 1.2: Mosques and minarets of Delhi.

Source: Author

Figure 1.3: Hindi notice board in an old Delhi mosque.

Source: Author

The use of *Sanskritized* Hindi in the inner domain and the adoption of global Islamic architectural features in the outer domain of mosques draw our attention to a complex Muslim identity. Obviously, we cannot say that reading the Quran in Hindi would 'Indianize' Delhi's Muslims, or installing a green minaret would make them global jihadis. These seemingly contradictory trends, I suggest, underline the making of a particular Muslim identity, which has not yet been fully conceptualized. What is important, from our point of view, is that we must acknowledge the fact that people who recognize themselves as Muslims do not find any contradiction in their self-perception as a religious ethnic group. But, when we put these experiences into a framework of research, this everydayness turns out to be a highly complicated phenomenon. Therefore, it is imperative for us to recognize the overlapping between identity as a lived experience and identity as an object of analysis as an intellectually productive vantage point.

III

Academic arguments and political positioning

Let us move to the second distinction that I make between the constitution of Muslim identities in public/political discourses and the study of Muslim identities in academic discourses. This distinction is perhaps problematic. Theoretically, it is almost impossible to detach political discourses from academic ones. Yet, this distinction is useful to make sense of the nature of public debates on Muslim identity.

It is important to note that Indian nationalism has produced an interesting category called 'public intellectuals'[17]—political elites not merely acted upon as politicians in the conventional sense of the term but also functioned as intellectuals and produced politically logical and intellectually persuasive arguments to mobilize people to their cause. There are many examples of this intellectual tradition. For instance, philosopher Mohammad Iqbal's famous poem 'Shikwa (*A Complaint*, 1909)' questions Allah's promise to protect Muslims, and B.R. Ambedkar's celebrated lecture 'Annihilation of Caste' were not meant for an academic public. Iqbal recited this controversial poem in a *mushaira* (symposium of poets) while Ambedkar was supposed to deliver this lecture in a public function.

Post-Partition Indian political realities posed challenges of very different kinds. Muslim identity, especially in the 1950s and 1960s, was either seen in the nationalism/separatism framework or in the traditional versus modernist framework. In fact, in 1964 when the so-called nationalist/modernist Muslims mainly associated with Congress attempted to form a pan-Indian Muslim consultative body called the All India Muslim Majlis-e-Mushawarat, they were criticized for encouraging separatism.[18]

This kind of Muslim identity formation in the public discourse evoked very interesting intellectual responses. The people who started working on Muslim communities argued that the study of non-Hindu societies in India could only illuminate the unity in diversity principle in the true sense. Sociologist Imtiaz Ahmad for example wrote in 1972:

> Greater attention must be paid to non-Hindu societies if our aim is to build a comprehensive sociology of India . . . [otherwise] . . . we may have Hindu, Muslim or Christian sociology, but hardly a sociology of India.[19]

This argument is simply a clear reflection on what may be called an agenda to bring non-Hindus (read Muslims) into the mainstream of academics. This quest for theoretically informed and empirically rich ethnographic work on Muslims paved the way for an intellectual position, which is often called the 'assimilation thesis'.[20] This thesis draws our attention to the diversity of Muslim communities intersected by religious, regional, linguistic, class, clan/caste and gendered differentials. This intellectual position was invoked not merely to respond to primordialists like Francis Robinson, who claims that Islam would remain the dominant source for not only Muslim politics but also communal leaders of all kinds. Ahmad wrote in 1981:

> Muslim fundamentalists may assert and maintain that there is one, only one version of what is orthodox from the Islamic point of view and whatever does not conform to it is to be dismissed as heterodox . . . Clearly it seems to me that Islamists' vision has tended to obscure the inherent and underlying pluralism within Indian Islam as a practised religion.[21]

The strength of Ahmad and others' argument was that they responded to the public debates on Muslim identity as well as certain academic stereotypes in intellectually sophisticated and methodologically rigorous ways. In fact, they evolved a political position and provided logical intellectual arguments in favour of it.

Ahmad's thesis on Muslim diversity, which was the outcome of a serious intellectual engagement with the communities, transformed into a dominant intellectual paradigm in later years. The debate on secularism in India reinvented this paradigm in an interesting manner in the 1990s.[22] After the demolition of the Babri Masjid in 1992, Indian politics was divided into two identifiable fractions: a dominant coalition of political parties, groups and intellectuals who described themselves as secular, and an emerging coalition of Hindutva forces that claimed to represent Hindu nationalist interests.[23] This political divide also directly impacted intellectual discourses, especially with regard to Muslims. The intellectual arguments that were produced mainly in relation to Muslim social stratifications and diversity were overstretched to justify an extremely vague and 'politically correct' notion of secularism.

Mushirul Hasan's book *Legacy of Divided Nation: India's Muslims Since Independence* (1997) is a relevant example in this regard. Criticizing Muslim politics of minority-ism practised by Muslim politicians and religious elites, Hasan talks about the Muslim liberal–modernist intelligentsia, who according to him, represents a truly secular Muslim culture. He writes:

> . . . the intelligentsia—artist and intellectual—creates mirrors through which we see ourselves and *windows* through which we perceive reality. It is these mirrors and windows that define the boundaries of ideas and institutions. The intelligentsia's role—both as creators of a cultural outlook and the product of the milieu—is central to this writer's view of what happened in India in general and among certain Muslim groups in particular.[24]

Hasan identifies three broad characteristics of these secular Muslims: these individuals fight to protect the basic Nehruvian model of Indian democracy; they believe that communalism and Hindu–Muslim strife need not imply the failure of secular experiments; and finally, they inherited these values from their nationalist–secular–progressive families.

The third characteristic of secular Muslim intelligentsia is very interesting. Hasan discusses the family background of these secular–modernists to highlight an 'Indian Muslim secular tradition'. Emphasizing the secular contribution of a few 'progressive' Muslim families, Hasan talks about the family of Mohammad Habib (Aligarh historian), and his brother, Mohammad Mujeeb, and Habib's son Irfan Habib, who contributed a lot to the secularization of India; the family of journalist Seema Mustafa, who is a part of the Kidwai clan, the home of Rafi Ahmad Kidwai. Her grandmother was a freedom fighter and social activist; the family of Hasan Suroor, a London-based journalist, whose father, despite being a British civil servant, was a Congress sympathizer and whose mother gave up her burqa (veil) to participate in social activities'.[25] Hasan concludes that these progressive Muslim secular intellectuals inherited secular values from their families and upheld the cause of secularism in India.

This description of secular–progressive Muslim intelligentsia as representative of 'Muslim secularism' is highly problematic. It seems that Hasan wants a few professionals, English-educated individuals/families to speak on behalf of Indian Muslim communities—primarily because of their expressed commitment to Nehruvian secularism. An argument of this kind goes well with the good Muslim–bad Muslim framework—an established template of Muslim politics in India.[26] In my view, Mushirul Hasan seems to deviate from the established procedure of research; instead, he relies heavily on the dominant political 'rhetoric of secularism' to justify his intellectual position as a Muslim secularist.[27] Unlike Imtiaz Ahmad, Hasan's political position remains elusive, vague and overtly rhetorical.

IV

Identity of a Muslim researcher

In 2001-02, Syed Ali, a US-based researcher conducted an ethnographic study of the Muslim caste system in Hyderabad. At the end of his article, he shared his fieldwork experience, he says:

> As a Muslim studying Muslims, I was privy to certain types of information that other ethnographers may not have had access to. But as a Syed, I was perhaps excluded from

certain types of information, since respondents may have assumed that I held some factional affiliation. I did not feel that my being a Syed excluded me, as no one I interacted with asked about my caste until I inquired about his or hers, which usually did not occur until well into the interviews. My caste was never a factor with people I interacted with more closely. I also had to fight the assumptions that because I am Hyderabadi (or at least my parents are), I understood the rituals and underlying social meaning of different events. Usually, this was not the case. I became jealous of white, Western ethnographers I met during field research because they were often treated better than me under the assumption that they were ignorant and needed to be instructed in detail. However, there were many things that I was privileged to be told or shown from which they were led away.[28]

Ali's statement underlines the point that I made in the Introduction that the Muslim identity of the researcher really matters in ethnographic fieldwork. But what is interesting in this account is the manner in which the researcher's own Muslim identity is reconstituted by the people, who were the subjects of analysis. It shows that the 'object' of research also reshapes the identity of a researcher.

This valuable inference, however, should not be taken as a 'ready to use formula'. One must be aware of an inherent theoretical problem associated with it, which may be called the 'experience syndrome'. There is a strong possibility that one begins to invoke his/her personal experiences as a Muslim researcher working on Muslim communities in an overtly autobiographical manner. It can be said that these Muslim experiences are unique and argumentatively justifiable. Although this position is fairly convincing, I find such assertions analytically unhelpful in two ways. First, individual experiences cannot be generalized. For instance, the experiences of a Muslim male researcher are going to be very different from a Muslim female researcher. They can certainly draw insights from each other's experiences. Yet, we cannot ignore the significance of factors like caste, class, and educational status of a researcher in determining the actual research encounters. The experience of being a Muslim and a Muslim researcher, hence, has its own limits. There is a second and more profound problem as well. If 'Muslim experiences' are recognized as a legitimate intellectual form to provide analytical coherence to the research narrative, why cannot this privilege be given to a Hindu researcher working on Hindu communities? After all, the Indian academic and political discourses have been suffering from the problem of 'competing victimhood' for a long time.

V

The contours of intellectual politics

Political theorist Peter DeSouza offers us an insightful argument to go beyond the experience syndrome. Problematizing the nature of intellectual work in the Indian context, he writes:

> The public intellectual has to carry both the persona of the autonomous intellectual and the advocate of social causes equally within himself or herself, sometimes allowing the one to dominate, sometimes the other. It is the tipping point that will determine when one yields to the other, when one recognizes in the political context the need for a particular persona to be in the foreground.[29]

The idea of a tipping point, in my view, needs to be elaborated. I find three possible expressions of it. First, we must 'distance' ourselves from the people/communities we research on. This creative-critical distancing is important because as researchers we are always in a privileged position. Our research output often gives us public visibility, professional gains and upward mobility. At the same time, we also have access to different sets of

information, which are not easily available to the communities/
participants we work on. Our academic/professional location,
in this sense, must be acknowledged; and precisely for this
reason, a creative-critical distance is always required to practice
what is often described as research ethics.

Secondly, we must pay close attention to the descriptive
aspects of our academic narratives. It is important to
emphasize that researchers interpret the communities/groups/
phenomenon by employing various hermeneutic strategies.
These interpretative exercises are not based on what a researcher
discovers in his/her research encounter; rather it is an outcome
of his/her analytical investment in the subject of research. Thus,
one must spell out the nature of these interpretative schemes for
the sake of intellectual transparency.

Finally, the nature of the arguments/conclusions we draw
from our research encounter is also very important. There is a
commonsensical view that intellectual/academic arguments are
delicate, tentative and open-ended; while political arguments/
positions are concrete and inflexible.[30] This distinction
is superficial and unhelpful. Deep engagement with any
phenomenon—intellectual or political—is bound to produce
argumentative openness. Gandhi's defence of his political
inconsistencies, for example, underlines the context-specific
nature of his intellectual arguments.[31] A researcher, therefore,
is expected to produce intellectually informed and politically
driven arguments in such a manner that his/her readers may be
able to draw their own political meanings.

This brings us back to the assertion that Irena Akbar poses:
'A Muslim must speak as a Muslim'. As a Muslim researcher,
my response is simple: I do not want to give up my identity as a
Muslim; yet, at the same time, I do not want to speak only as a
Muslim. I practice intellectual politics that encourages me to take
a political position without compromising with the established
protocols, procedures and ethics of my profession as an academic.[32]

Chapter 2

What Is *New* in New India?

I

New India and its constitutionalism

To understand the placing of Muslim identity in the framework of 'New India', we need to carefully look at this doctrine in its entirety.[1] More specifically, we must examine the nature of the structural–political changes introduced by the Modi regime after 2014. These changes have redefined the political context in a significant way. The contemporary political reconfiguration of Muslim identity is an outcome of this crucial process.

New India is a well-worked-out ideological framework. It was first introduced as a political slogan by Prime Minister Narendra Modi in his 2017 Independence Day speech.[2] Highlighting the need to have a positive outlook, Modi argued: 'If each one of us . . . strives with a new resolve, a new energy, a new strength, we can change the face of the country with our combined strength in the 75th year of our independence in 2022.'[3] The BJP formally accepted the idea of New India as a political principle in 2018.[4] This formal recognition led to an official campaign to seek citizens' participation in this initiative. The Niti Aayog brought out an interesting document, *Strategy*

17

for New India @ 75 which outlines a policy framework to translate the doctrine of New India into a workable action plan.[5]

Narendra Modi's official website introduces us to the three core features of New India: a nation driven by innovation, hard work and creativity; a nation characterized by peace, unity and brotherhood; a country free from corruption, terrorism, black money and dirt.[6] To realize these goals, citizens of India are asked to take a nine-point pledge to express their commitment and faith in the doctrine of New India. This is an interesting pledge. On one hand, the citizens are expected to support and participate actively in official programmes such as Swachh Bharat, Accessible India and the cashless economy. On the other hand, the government does not take any responsibility to provide employment to citizens. In fact, seeking employment as a right is strongly discouraged. Citizens are told that job creation is not a duty of the government. The last theme of the New India pledge reiterates this point more sharply. It says: 'I will be a job creator not a job seeker.'[7]

The state in New India, in this sense, seems to assert itself as a sovereign entity to work on behalf of the citizens in the sphere of politics; while, at the same time, it keeps itself away from the economic sphere and does not take any responsibility on behalf of citizens. For Modi, 'New India is the era of responsive people and responsive government.'[8] (emphasis mine)

To understand the political implications of this 'responsive government-responsive people' formulation, we have to look at the ways in which the doctrine of New India is linked to what I call 'Hindutva constitutionalism'.

There can be two meanings of the term 'constitutionalism'. In a rather technical sense, constitutionalism refers to the norms and principles that not only create state institutions (legislative, executive and judicial powers) but also impose certain limits and curbs on them. Hence, constitutionalism as a positive principle reminds the political elites to follow the legal limits set out by the Constitution.[9] However, there is a political meaning of constitutionalism in the Indian context that has evolved over the years.[10] The ideologically divided political class of the 1950s somehow accepted the Constitution as the fundamental reference point to participate in formal electoral politics. Yet, there was a strong apprehension about the success of the Constitution in the Indian context. This led to an interesting ideological churning. Political parties relied heavily on the language of constitutionalism in the realm of electoral politics. On the other hand, they continued to evolve different ideologically suitable interpretations of the Indian Constitution. This intellectual engagement with the Constitution actually paved the way for various kinds of ideologically oriented and politically feasible constitutionalism. Hindutva constitutionalism is one such political form.[11]

It is important to remember that the Hindutva groups never envisaged the Constitution as a self-explanatory text. In the post-1990 period, every political party, including the left groups, started celebrating the Indian Constitution as the ultimate symbol of Indian democracy. Even the Vajpayee government constituted a committee to evaluate and review the workings of the Constitution (the National Commission to review the working of the Constitution [NCRWC] also known as Venkatachaliah Commission).[12] The BJP, however, changed its attitude in the 2010s. The party started employing the Constitution's potential for its Hindutva politics in two significant ways.

First of all, the Constitution was transformed into a sacred political object. The prime ministerial candidate of the BJP, Narendra Modi, began his 2014 election campaign with a bold declaration that the 'Constitution is a 'holy book' and that the only code of conduct of the government should be

'Sabka Saath, Sabka Vikas'.[13] This fascination with the Constitution as a sacred political object took a more formal shape after the success of the BJP in the 2014 election. In October 2015, the Modi government declared that 26 November, the day when the Constituent Assembly adopted the final draft of the Constitution in 1949, would be celebrated as 'Samvidhan Divas' (Constitution Day) every year. In a speech dedicated to the greatness of the Constitution, Modi went on to say that ' . . . if there is any creation made by man, which is immortal, it's India's Constitution'.[14]

There was another very crucial and thoughtful move by the BJP leadership. Senior BJP leaders, especially Narendra Modi and Amit Shah, did not use the expression 'Hindutva' to describe the nature of their politics. Unlike L.K. Advani or A.B. Vajpayee, who celebrated Hindutva as a reflection of cultural nationalism, Narendra Modi always stays away from any direct discussion on this issue.[15] The speech he delivered on 3 December 2018 in Rajasthan is the best example to underline this point. Responding to Rahul Gandhi's allegation that Narendra Modi did not have true knowledge of Hindutva, he replied:

> He says Modi has no knowledge of Hinduism. Oh brother, is it an electoral issue? . . . Rajasthan needs to vote on the issues such as electricity, roads, and water. It has nothing to do with Modi's knowledge of Hindu; I don't understand this . . . However, I will definitely say that our culture is a storehouse of knowledge . . . and Hindutva . . . is a rich heritage. This Hindutva, this Hindu knowledge is so profound . . . so vast, and so ancient . . . it is higher than the Himalayas and deeper than the sea. No one can claim that he or she has complete knowledge of it. Even the sages never claimed to have full knowledge of Hindu and Hindutva. I am a very small man and I do not claim to have such a vast knowledge.[16]

Modi does not find it logical to compare Hindutva with material/developmental issues. He does not even make the conventional argument that Hindutva is a way of life, and it has nothing to do with politics. Modi actually conceptualizes Hindutva as an uncontested, neutral and self-evident cultural expression of Indian identity. In other words, Modi, unlike Advani, does not express regret that Hindutva is misunderstood or eventually linked to the BJP's politics. Instead, he confidently asserts that there is no need to discuss Hindutva in the realm of politics as it has become a new political commonness. This strong claim might have been the reason why the BJP officially did not describe Hindutva as its core political philosophy after 2012.[17]

These two moves—Hindutva as an acceptable cultural idiom and the Constitution as a sacred political object—have actually constituted Hindutva constitutionalism: a political mechanism that is created to achieve the 'responsive people and responsive government' thesis.[18]

Three core features of Hindutva constitutionalism are relevant to our discussion. First of all, there is a strong adherence to legal technicalities to articulate a politically favourable position. Hindutva groups make a crucial distinction between the political–philosophical principles that the Constitution invokes (such as secularism, rule of law, liberty and rights) and the legal technicalities associated with them. The constitutional principles are celebrated as fixed, settled and static ideals; while the legal technicalities are seen as 'matters of concern', which need to be amended and rationalized.[19] This framework helps the Hindutva groups, especially the BJP, to emphasize on the rights of the state and the Fundamental Duties of the citizens. This is precisely what Narendra Modi calls the 'paradigm shift'. He argues:

For some reason everything was centred around (sic) rights. Everyone was concerned with rights. This is an opportunity whereby we can ensure a paradigm shift within the country by carrying it towards duties from rights. The responsibility of the people's representatives is also to awaken the people's conscience and to lead the way.[20]

Emphasis on a refined and more profound idea of minority—not majority—is the second feature of Hindutva constitutionalism. In the last six years, Hindutva groups have tried to appropriate the idea of minority to legitimize the 'Hindu victimhood' argument.[21] A BJP leader in 2017 filed a public interest litigation (PIL) in the Supreme Court, demanding that Hindus must be declared a minority in eight states and Union Territories (Lakshadweep, Mizoram, Nagaland, Meghalaya, Jammu and Kashmir, Arunachal Pradesh, Manipur and Punjab). It is claimed that the minority rights of Hindus are 'being siphoned off illegally and arbitrarily to the majority population because neither Central nor the State Governments have notified . . . Hindus as a "minority" in these states'.[22] The CAA, 2019 also extends the scope of this legal claim. By highlighting the persecution of Hindu minorities in Muslim states in neighbouring countries, this law seems to underline the old RSS argument: the Hindu majority in India is insignificant because India is surrounded by Muslim-majority states. To address this problem of numbers, the Hindutva groups offer a simple yet highly provocative solution. It is suggested that majority-minority distinction must be abolished to create a national political community of citizens. The slogan 'development for all and appeasement of none' actually stems from this refined Hindutva imagination.[23]

Finally, Hindutva constitutionalism recognizes 'one nation-one Constitution' as the foundational principle of its politics. Instead of relying entirely on the conventional Hindu nationalist argument that Kashmir—a Muslim-majority state—should not have any special status, the Hindutva groups propose a refined legal explanation. It is asserted that while the other provisions of the Constitution are fixed, permanent and consistent, Article 370 is an unwanted and useless addition to it. BJP's political determination and Modi–Shah's strong will, according to this line of reasoning, have been instrumental in achieving the one nation–one Constitution framework.[24] It is worth noting that the presidential order that revoked the special status of Kashmir is called 'The Constitution (Application to Jammu and Kashmir) Order, 2019'.

II

New India as the 'mother of democracy'

The government of India introduced a new official theme 'India: The Mother of Democracy' to commemorate the Constitution Day on 26 November 2022. According to the official circular issued by the Ministry of Education, academic and educational institutions were directed to undertake activities such as the collective readings of the Preamble of the Constitution and organizing webinars/seminars and quiz competitions on this theme.[25] A Concept Note prepared by the Indian Council of Historical Research (ICHR) in English, 'Bharat: Loktantra ki Janani', was also circulated with this official order to provide a broad overview of this new thematic concern.[26] The ICHR later published an edited volume entitled *India: The Mother of Democracy* as a reference book in this regard.

This initiative was widely publicized. Prime Minister Narendra Modi explained the meanings of this phrase in his *Mann ki Baat*. He said:

> . . . we Indians are also proud of the fact that our country is also the Mother of Democracy. Democracy is in our veins; it is in our culture—it has been an integral part of our

work for centuries. By nature, we are a Democratic Society. Dr Ambedkar had compared the Buddhist monks' union to the Indian Parliament . . . Babasaheb believed that Lord Buddha must have got inspiration from the political systems of that time.[27]

It is worth noting that ICHR's Concept Note does not have any direct reference to Buddhism or B.R. Ambedkar. Instead, it addresses the Indian tradition of democracy as a reflection of 'Hindu political theory'. This one-sided representation of Indian political traditions was criticized by a few serious scholars.[28] It is argued that the Concept Note is based on the Hindutva framework of history, and it aims to establish RSS's perception of India's past. It is also argued that the Concept Note ignores alternative historical traditions and does not encourage critical thinking.[29]

There is certainly merit in this kind of criticism. However, I do not think that this Concept Note should entirely be rejected as a political pamphlet of some kind. This Note opens the possibility of rethinking those historical foundations that have led to the success of democracy in India. At the same time, it asks us to pay close attention to the grassroots cultures and subaltern imaginations so as to capture the ethos of democracy in the Indian context. Precisely for this reason, there is a need to engage with this Concept Note intellectually.

The Concept Note makes two broad claims. It begins with a very clear and straightforward question of translation. Comparing a few popular Hindi expressions, an attempt is made to extract the context-specific meanings of democracy. It says:

A distinction needs to be drawn between Praja-Tantra, Jana-Tantra, and Loka-Tantra. One is a straight translation of the political system known as 'Democracy', the second is

'People versus the ruler(s) oriented system', and the third is 'a community-system oriented towards the welfare of the community'.

In order to establish the *Loka-Tantra* as an Indian version of democracy or the 'people's polity', the Note describes three universally accepted features: (i) limits on the Ruler(s); (ii) accountability of the Ruler(s); (iii) people's direct or indirect partition in governance and/or their rights of self-governance. These three features, it is argued, correspond to the Loka-Tantra in a historical sense and paved the way for what is called the 'Indian form of governance'.[30] It is claimed:

> In India, from the Vedic times itself, two kinds of states, *Janapada* and *Rajya* have been in the existence. The Indian experience evolved its own form of governance at the levels of the village and the central polity: (i) the federal/central political structures were delinked from the life of the community (village communities), and consequently (ii) village communities became self-governing and autonomous, and (iii) developed a hierarchy of self-governing institutions, such as panchayat and khaps, that enabled them to remain unaffected by and large by the changing kingdoms/empires particularly those of the invaders hostile to Hindu culture.

The framing of this intellectual claim is conceptually problematic. It begins with the premise that the idea of democracy needs to be historicized. This historicization, however, is not taken as any kind of theoretical challenge. The three identified features of democracy are presented to us as universally accepted ahistorical/apolitical attributes. The Note does not tell how the presence of self-governing institutions ensured the first two features of democracy in the Indian context, namely the limits on the ruler, and his/her accountability.

At the same time, the Note fails to clarify the crucial distinction between democracy and governance. We are left with a few puzzling questions: if *Janapada* and *Rajya* were delinked, what was the relationship between the self-governing grassroots subaltern institutions and the central polity? What is the significance of the term 'hostile invaders' in this framework? Does it mean that the desecration of Hindu temples by the non-Hindu invaders was a political act that was directly related to the Rajyas, not Janapadas?

Instead of clarifying such issues, the Concept Note makes a second powerful claim:

> This explains the survival of Hindu culture and civilization in the face of 2000 years of invasions by alien ethnicities and cultures. This became possible because the Hindu mind from the beginning addressed the central question of how to wield this vast multiplicity that is India into a single larger community and from ancient times a geo-cultural definition has been given to this entity, Rashtra, Bharata—the country which lies to the south of the Himalayas and the north of the ocean is called Bharata and the Bhartiyas are the people of this country.

This statement goes against the very logic of historicization. The Note wants us to believe that terms like 'Hindu mind', 'Bharat' and 'Bhartiyata' have been fixed, static and unchangeable for over 2000 years. This historical reductionism is evoked to justify the territory-centric imaginations of the Hindu nation and its political organization. An impression is created that the Hindu, and for that matter, non-Hindu, constitutes the prime contradiction of Indian past and present: Hindus are democratic by nature (even if they belong to Rajya!) hence, they are the parents of democracy; while non-Hindus can legitimately be called invaders or anti-democratic (even if they are intermingled culturally in the realms of Janapada/Panchayats) and hence, there is no need to study them.

This intellectual inconsistency needs to be addressed in its entirety. The success of democracy in India is a political question that can only be answered politically. Precisely for this reason, there is a need to understand the nature of the political narrative that has produced this rather complicated and seemingly incorrect imagination of democracy.

III

New India and the narratives of Indian politics

Congress leader Jairam Ramesh made an interesting point while commenting on the success of the party's flagship campaign, Bharat Jodo Yatra (BJY). He said, ' . . . through BJY . . . we have succeeded . . . to set the terms of debate and the narrative in the political discourse.'[31]

Ramesh, like many other serious non-BJP politicians, employs the term 'narrative' to underline the contested nature of public debates, especially in the electoral arena. Although he did not use the word Hindutva in this interview, he acknowledged the capacity of the BJP to set the conditions for a particular kind of ideas to survive in public discussions. BJY, in his view, is a crucial event that has given Congress an opportunity to get rid of this given framework. In other words, an 'alternative narrative' of politics is being unfolded.

No one can deny the significance of this political comment. It is true that the Congress, as the main opposition party, has come out with an original and constructive idea of Yatra to carve out an intellectual space for itself in the Hindutva-dominated political environment. The active participation of liberal and progressive intellectuals, civil society organizations and representatives of the people's movements has also contributed significantly to this process. It will be too early to make a conclusive remark on the outcome of this Yatra. Yet, Ramesh's comment offers us an opportunity to briefly explore different postcolonial political narratives that have evolved in specific historical contexts.

The term 'narrative', and for that matter 'political narrative', is used very freely to convey several different and even contradictory expressions. It is, therefore, important to underline the specific sense in which it is used in contemporary Indian public life.

In my view, a political narrative could be described as a form of communication between political parties and the citizens. It aims to explain political realities by arranging a set of identified issues, events and key figures in a particular sequence. Three essential elements of our public life are relevant in this regard: the legal–constitutional structures, changing policy framework and electoral mobilization. These elements are used as resources by the political parties to create favourable electoral packages to attract voters in the electoral arena.

A political narrative becomes successful only when it is accepted by the entire political class as an essential and unavoidable reference point for political communication. For instance, 'socialism' was the dominant narrative in the first few decades after the Independence. It was gradually replaced by the narrative of 'secularism' in the mid-1980s when even the BJP started celebrating its philosophy of cultural nationalism as 'real secularism'.[32] In the 2000s, a new narrative of 'inclusion' became the buzzword for political transactions. However, it faded away by the early 2010s, especially after the India Against Corruption movement, which led to the formation of the AAP. Consequently, 'nationalism' has emerged as the decisive narrative of politics.

Socialism was the first dominant narrative of Indian politics. It began to take a concrete shape in the 1940s itself. Although the word 'Socialist' was not included in the Preamble of the original Constitution, it was one of the most seriously discussed themes in the Constituent Assembly. The outcome was obvious: the Constitution was not officially socialist, yet it was committed to the idea of social justice and economic equality.

The first general election was an interesting experiment at the ideological level as well. The success of the Congress, communists and the socialists in the 1952 elections forced all political players to recognize socialism as a reference point to reconfigure their future ideological positions. The Congress adopted Nehruvian doctrine, the *socialistic pattern of society*; the Communist Party followed the ideal of 'people's democracy' to achieve socialism; and thinkers like Ram Manohar Lohia and Jayaprakash Narayan made serious attempts to redefine socialism in the Indian context. Interestingly, parties like Bhartiya Jan Sangh (BJS), which were committed to Hindu nationalism, also recognized socialism as an important consideration. In fact, Deendayal Upadhyaya described 'socialism as a force' to claim that BJS was '. . . socialist in its emotional and ideational appeal.'[33]

The Emergency period (1975–77) was perhaps the most significant moment in this regard. Indira Gandhi regime amended the Constitution to formally insert the term 'socialist' in the Preamble. This move helped the Congress government to legitimize its authoritarian policies without deviating from the acceptable narrative of politics.

A few critical events of the 1980s—the assassination of Indira Gandhi, the Shah Bano case and the Babri Masjid–Ram Janmabhoomi controversy—destabilized the narrative of socialism. Although socialism as a concept continued to survive, the political class found it rather irrelevant to deal with the growing influence of religion in public life.

Around the same time, the policy framework also went through a decisive change. The market economy and liberalization were accepted as the ultimate form of economic system in the 1990s. This new political consensus in favour of the market in a way transformed the state into a 'mediating' agency to resolve societal conflicts.

In this highly volatile context, secularism emerged as the new dominant narrative of Indian politics. The Congress established itself as the leader of the secular camp after the demolition of the Babri Masjid in 1992. The BJP and Shiv Sena were symbolized as communal parties in this schema. Interestingly, the BJP also accepted secularism as a point of reference to legitimize itself, especially in the domain of electoral politics. Criticizing the secularism of the secular parties as 'pseudo-secularism', the BJP leaders made a strong claim in favour of what they called 'secularism without appeasement'.[34]

The narrative of secularism started fading away during the late 1990s. The BJP gave up three controversial issues—Ram Temple, Uniform Civil Code (UCC) and Article 370—to lead the National Democratic Alliance (NDA).[35] On the other hand, the non-NDA forces were desperate to evolve a broad ideological consensus that could give them a new language to survive in the electoral arena.

The 2004 election was a turning point. Secularism was not given up completely by the newly formed United Progressive Alliance (UPA) government. Instead, it was redefined as one of the constituents of what was called 'politics of social justice and inclusiveness'. It paved the way for the third dominant narrative of politics—inclusion. This narrative was based on the premise that the marginalized social groups—women, children, Dalits, Adivasis, unorganized labour, minorities/Muslims and so on—were to be seen as stakeholders. In this schema, the state was envisaged as an agency to facilitate welfarism as sectoral 'empowerment' in such a way that the commitment to the free market could not be compromised.

The narrative of inclusion was rather short-lived. The anti-corruption movement of 2011, followed by the protests about the gang-rape in Delhi in 2012 were the watershed events. Nationalism made a decisive comeback in these protests. The national flag, copy of the Constitution and images of national figures were used by the protestors to argue that the country needed a truly nationalist government. This wider acceptability of nationalism had two very clear manifestations. The newly formed Aam Aadmi Party (AAP) defined nationalism in terms of service delivery; while BJP introduced Narendra Modi as the 'decisive leader' to reclaim nationalism in overtly Hindutva terms. The electoral success of the BJP in the post-2014 period has helped Hindutva-driven nationalism to become the contemporary narrative of Indian politics.

These four clearly identifiable narratives—socialism, secularism, inclusion and Hindutva-driven nationalism—dominate, survive, overlap and compete with each other in the real world of politics. The doctrine of New India is an outcome of this contestation.

IV

New India and the charitable state

There is also a huge challenge before the new India. If attention is not paid now, it can cause a lot of damage to the youth of India and today's generation. Your present will go astray, and your future will be confined to darkness, friends. That is why it is important to wake up now. Nowadays, every effort is being made in our country to introduce the culture of collecting votes by distributing freebies. This culture of freebies is very dangerous for the development of the country. The people of the country and especially my youth need to be very careful of this freebies culture. The people following this culture will never build new expressways, airports or defence corridors for you. They feel that they will buy the people by distributing freebies to them. Together we have to defeat this approach and remove the freebies culture from the politics of the country.[36]

Prime Minister Narendra Modi made this statement criticizing what he called the 'freebies culture' (or *revdi* culture). This criticism, interestingly, was interpreted in two very contradictory ways. A section of political observers found Modi's statement rather strange. The freebies, described as an important aspect of India's political economy, have also helped the BJP.[37] This inference, in a way, is empirically justifiable. The party has relied heavily on populist welfare schemes to attract voters in recent elections.

On the other hand, Modi's comment was also appreciated enthusiastically. It was seen as a serious political assessment that delineates the long-term impact of freebies culture on the economic life of the country.[38] This line of argument justifies Modi's assertion by making a crucial distinction between 'revdi culture' and authentic welfarism. These two conflicting interpretations, it seems, focus entirely on the most provocative expression of Modi's speech, the revdi culture and somehow do not pay any attention to some of the serious structural issues, which Narendra Modi underlined.[39]

A careful reading of Modi's speech reveals that he was actually trying to redefine the idea of social justice to accommodate it in his doctrine of New India. More specifically, there was an attempt to specify the contours of what I call the 'charitable state': a pro-market state that provides some facilities to citizens on a case-to-case basis; and, at the same time, bargains with them in the realm of competitive electoral politics.

To understand the wider implications of Modi's speech, one must look at the political context in which the notion of a charitable state has evolved in India. The Constitution describes 'welfarism' as a political duty of the state simply to recognize citizens as rights-bearing stakeholders. This constitutional imagination, however, has been significantly redefined by successive governments in the last three decades.

The political class's enthusiasm to accept the market economy as the ultimate form of the economic system in the 1990s led to a new political consensus. A strong impression was created that the open market framework did not need any state intervention. The function of the state, therefore, was restricted to the political sphere. This imagination of the state–economy relationship was uncritically accepted by all political parties. As a result, the state began to redefine itself as a 'mediating agency' to resolve societal conflicts while maintaining a distance from the economic sphere.

This framework paved the way for a sectoral approach to the idea of welfare, especially under the UPA regime of 2004–14. The social groups—women, children, Dalits, Adivasis, unorganized labour, minorities/Muslims and so on—were seen as stakeholders of social justice to characterize welfarism as sectoral 'empowerment'.

Modi-led BJP has given new meanings to this imagination of welfarism without deviating from the national political consensus on open market and sectoral empowerment. It has made a serious effort to reach out to the concerned individuals, the labharthis (beneficiaries), for direct and effective political transactions. Modi's criticism of the culture of freebies actually stems from the BJP's version of the charitable state. Four clearly identifiable aspects of Modi's speech in Bundelkhand are relevant to elaborate on this point.

First, Modi rejects the culture of freebies based on his imagination of 'responsive citizens'. The doctrine of New India, as we have shown in the first section of this chapter, is based on a direct correlation between 'responsive government and responsive citizens'. In this schema, the citizen is seen as a duty-bound entity. Explaining the idea of responsive citizens, Home Minister Amit Shah also made a very similar argument. He said, 'There is a difference in the way we work: we have given gas connections, power connections and it's up to them to pay their bills. We have made toilets for them but they have to maintain them . . . when you take populist measures, you promise to pay electricity bills, free gas etc. What we did was to provide help to upgrade their lives—this is empowerment.'[40] Modi also reiterated this point in his speech. As previously stated, he asserted that the 'culture of freebies is very dangerous for the development of the country . . . and the people . . . especially youth need to be very careful of this . . . The double-engine governments are not adopting the shortcut of distributing freebies, but they are working hard to improve the future.'

Second, the responsive government-responsive citizen framework also makes it possible for Modi to make an intelligent connection between populist schemes and large-scale infrastructure projects. Criticising the non-BJP parties, Modi argued that those who follow the freebies culture, 'will never build new expressways, airports or defence corridors for you. They feel that they will buy the people by distributing freebies to them.'[41] This is a very important point of departure. The charitable state actually functions as a 'facilitator' to the open market by creating an infrastructure for its smooth functioning. The welfare schemes targeting the individual labharthis are to be described as an extension of this receptive developmental agenda.

Modi also made this point. He said, 'Instead of the freebies culture, we are working to fulfil the aspirations of the people by building roads and new rail routes in the country.

We are building crores of pucca houses for the poor, completing unfinished irrigation projects for decades, constructing many small and big dams, setting up new electricity plants so that the life of the poor and the farmer becomes easier.'[42]

Third, Modi tries to unpack the political capabilities associated with the notion of social justice. Instead of defining social justice purely in terms of identity-based exclusions (religious, caste and gender), he offered a development-oriented conceptualization. Evoking the regional imbalance, especially in eastern India and the Bundelkhand region of Uttar Pradesh, Modi argued that infrastructural development in a backward region must also be seen as a kind of social justice. For him, 'balanced development of the country and access to modern facilities even in small towns and villages also amounts to social justice in true sense'.[43]

This brings us to the fourth point, the idea of political 'bargaining'—a key feature of the charitable state model. Modi criticized the Opposition for preserving the culture of freebies. It does not, however, mean that he gave up this idea of political bargain completely. If we carefully read this speech, we find a very different and intelligent proposal. Modi urged the citizens to recognize the capabilities of a 'double-engine' government that would give them recognition, infrastructure, and above all, individual-centric benefits.

The question arises: is the doctrine of New India, especially the meanings it offers to Indian democracy, citizenship and welfarism, strictly confined to the politics of the BJP? Or has it become an avoidable reference point for a wider political consensus? We shall explore this question systematically in the next few chapters.

Chapter 3

New India and the Muslim *Historical*

I

What is *Amrit Kaal?*

Prime Minister Narendra Modi's 2023 Independence Day speech was called flat and unexciting.[1] In a way, this speech dissatisfied two very different kinds of political observers. It did not offer any new mantra to Modi's admirers. Except for the slogan, 'demography, democracy and diversity', Modi did not make any different, extraordinary, or unexpected claim, which could further be highlighted as a 'masterstroke' by a section of pro-BJP media.

On the other hand, the speech was disappointing for Modi's opponents as well. Modi was not in 'campaign mode'. His condemnation of the Opposition was implicit and thematic. Without naming any political party, he criticized the dynastic rule—the dominance of one particular family—as an undemocratic phenomenon. This careful criticism obviously does not offer any possibility for Modi's rivals to use this speech as a political resource.

Yet, this was one of the most important political statements Modi has made in the last ten years as the prime minister of this country.[2] The speech was not delivered for direct media consumption. Instead, it was a serious attempt to provide a functional thematic outline to the structural–political changes introduced by the Modi regime after 2014. More specifically, this speech introduces us to the idea of 'political time', which goes beyond the BJP's well-known criticism of Indian history. Modi not merely made an effort to establish a link between the past and the present but also tried to offer a different imagination of the political future. Precisely for this reason, we should look at it carefully.

Modi evokes the idea of political time to offer an interesting classificatory schema. The Indian past is divided into two overlapping categories—the period of slavery and the period of struggle and liberation; while India's present (and future!) is described as the *Amrit Kaal*.

The speech begins with here and now, especially with a minor reference to Manipur violence. This present is located in a different timespan—the period of slavery that began around 1000–1200 years ago. Modi argues that the defeat of one small kingdom at that time was not an insignificant event. According to him, this defeat caused serious damage and somehow paved the way for cultural and political subjugation. There was no specific mention of any ruler or kingdom in this formulation. Yet, Modi was able to communicate the standard Hindutva criticism of secular history, which makes a crucial distinction between the empires established by Muslim rulers and modern British colonialism.[3]

It does not mean that Modi completely ignores this distinction. His formulation recognizes the political significance of the national movement in a slightly different way. The struggle against British colonialism, he claims, marks the period of struggle and liberation. Modi argues that the struggle for freedom, which started almost a thousand years ago, found a new political overtone during the anti-British national movement. The political independence, that India achieved in 1947, was the successful outcome of this long and uninterrupted freedom struggle.

According to Modi, the contemporary time may be called the Amrit Kaal. Unlike the polemical claims often made by a section of pro-BJP media, Modi does not recognize 2014 as a decisive point of time to mark the beginning of Amrit Kaal. In his schema, the Amrit Kaal has just begun. He says:

> I am talking about the events of a thousand years ago for a reason. I am witnessing another opportunity before our country, a time when we are living in such a period, when we have entered such an era. It is our good fortune that either we are living in youth or we have taken birth in the lap of Mother India in the first year of 'Amrit Kaal'. And mark my words, my dear family members, the actions we take, the steps we take, the sacrifices we make, the penance we undertake in this era will define our legacy.[4]

It means that our political time not merely symbolizes our present, it is also a decisive moment to enter into a new political future.

Modi conceptualizes two versions of this political future—an immediate future, which is near and foreseeable and a long-term future, which is still imagined and yet attainable. He expresses his confidence that the immediate future is almost controllable. The statement that he would be delivering the next Independence Day speech in 2024 (which assumes he will win the 2024 elections) underlines this confidence. The long-term term future—India of 2047—however, is described concerning three challenges: dynastic politics, corruption and appeasement.

One may underline a few obvious limitations of this speech, especially the neat and clean categorization of political time into 'caged past' and 'liberated present'. Modi did not talk about the crucial period of our postcolonial experiences, which transformed India into a powerful global player. Nor did he touch upon the period when the BJP was ruling the country a little more than two decades ago and in fact, he himself was the chief minister of Gujarat.

These factual criticisms are politically insignificant. Modi is not writing a logical-factual history of India's past. Instead, he is interested in the present moment of our political time. And for this reason, Amrit Kaal is presented to us as an empty template, which has to be filled by 'political actions' and 'performances'. Obviously, there is nothing on the Muslim past in it directly. Yet, this classification of political time sets out a serious discourse in which Muslimness will always remain a contested entity.

II

New India and the Hindu pride of liberals

Hindutva's unease with secular history, and for that matter, with the Muslim past, is clearly understandable. It does not, however, mean that the position of the non-Hindutva political forces on the Muslim past is a settled issue. One finds that a new version of '*Garv se kaho hum Hindu hai* [State proudly that we are Hindus]' slogan of the 1980s is taking a concrete shape in the writings of a section of non-BJP intellectuals as well. These scholars claim to counter the hegemony of Hindutva by 'discovering' a true, authentic and historical Hinduism. They are also critical of the secular view of the Indian past, and for that reason, work overtime to 'liberate' Hindus and Hinduism from the Nehruvian elite and 'biased' Marxist historians. Shashi Tharoor, a well-known author and diplomat famous for his intellectual frankness, suddenly becomes a 'proud Hindu' and writes *Why I am a Hindu?*.[5] Pavan K. Varma, another diplomat, who once admired the Mughal empire, especially Akbar and Dara Shikoh, as a symbol of Hindu–Muslim unity in his first book *Ghalib: The Man, The Times,*[6] also realizes that he belongs to a great Hinduism that has nothing to do with Akbar or Ghalib. His position is articulated in *The Great Hindu Civilization: Achievement, Neglect, Bias and the Way Forward (2021)*.

There is nothing wrong in accepting Hinduism as an important identity marker. These scholars cannot and should not be blamed for offering a critique of BJP's Hindutva. But there is a problem. Their rather elusive search for 'Hindu civilization', interestingly, does not provide any legitimate space for Muslim identity. They reproduce the Hindutva-inspired history of Hindu subjugation and victimhood. This intellectualism is more dangerous because it silently excludes Muslims in the name of imaginary anti-BJPism.

Let us examine Pavan K. Varma's book, *The Great Hindu Civilization: Achievement, Neglect, Bias and the Way Forward* (2021) and Shashi Tharoor's *Why I am Hindu?* (2018) in some detail as examples of this new intellectual trend. These books address a particular section of readers—English-educated, academic-oriented, sympathetic to the Hindu cultural past and dissatisfied with Hindutva—and claim to offer an intellectual argument for it.

Varma begins his exploration with a noble claim: ' . . . In spite of the negative that it acquired over a period, the Hindu civilization is without parallel in the world for the sheer robustness of its cerebration, and the creative output that is its consequences.'[7]

He traces the success of this great Hindu culture to its authenticity. For him, the advent of Islam in India was an objectionable historical fact that broke the unadulterated flow of the pure Hindu past. Varma writes:

> The conquest of India by foreigners starting with the seventeen invasions of Mahmood Ghazni . . . left Hindu India physically destroyed and psychologically traumatized . . . Hindu civilization had never seen conquerors like the Islamic . . . invaders, who blindly committed to the destruction of a culture.[8]

Tharoor makes a similar point:

> . . . for invaders like Mahmud of Ghazni the attacks had twin motives the fabled wealth of India was mostly hoarded in its temples, which made them attractive targets, but there was also the zeal of the Muslim warrior to smash the seats of idolatry. The Hindus were left with a stark choice: revive or disappear. Renewal was the Hindu response.[9]

These observations remind us of the nineteenth-century colonial officials' writings, which always described India as a 'zone of conflict'. It seems Varma, who claims to be very critical of British Orientalism, not merely accepted the colonial view of Islam as a destructive force but also asserted it quite stridently to make a case for the purity of the Hindu past.

Tharoor is almost silent on the impact of Sufism. He makes a few passing references to Sufism in his book to show Hindu openness. Varma, however, is very critical of Sufi traditions. He envisages it as an Islamic conspiracy to subjugate Hindus with the support of Muslim rulers. He writes:

> Sufism . . . was greatly influenced by Hindu metaphysics and Bhakti movement . . . But, the Sufi faith never rejected Islam and many of its leading figures were vocal supporters—as in

case of Amir Khusro—of the religious iconoclasm practiced
by Muslim rulers.[10]

This reductionist view of Sufism is historically misleading and
culturally problematic. Varma is seemingly unaware of the
great contribution of Shail Mayaram to Mewati communities.
Mayaram argues that it was very difficult for the colonial
regime to classify communities based on Hinduism and Islam
in the Mewat region.[11] Sufiism stands for a 'lived religiosity'
that evolved in medieval India. Varma's Hindu essentialism
does not have space for it.

Relying on his version of Hindu history, Varma offers us a
highly one-sided view of Muslim politics in colonial India. For
him, there is a direct relationship between the establishment of
educational institutions such as Deoband and Aligarh in the
nineteenth century and the political demands of the Muslim
League in the 1940s. He notes:

> The conservative Deoband seminary opened in 1866 with . . .
> [the] aim of spearheading Muslim revivalism . . . In 1906 a
> delegation of Muslim leaders met Lord Minto and demanded
> separate electorate . . . In 1930 . . . poet Mohammed Iqbal
> clearly spoke of the idea of a separate nation . . . In 1940
> the Muslim League led by . . . Jinnah passed a resolution
> for the creation of Pakistan. The inevitable happened in
> 1947, and Bharat, that is India, was partitioned to create two
> separate states.[12]

This highly insubstantial description of Muslim politics creates
an impression that it was actually Muslims alone and all Muslims
without exception who were responsible for the partition of
Hindu Bharat. Varma fails to recognize the crucial distinction
between the political aspiration of Muslim communities and the
high politics of the Muslim elite.[13] Besides, the role of Hindu

communal organizations, such as Hindu Mahasabha, are not given any attention. Tharoor, however, does not get into this complicated historical business and evokes the Partition merely to underline the point that BJP is transforming Indian into a 'Hindu Pakistan'.[14]

These three features of Muslim presence construct a very hostile image of contemporary Muslim communities. Muslims are presented as children of invaders, adherents of an alien 'unspiritual' faith and the real culprits of Partition. Varma does not offer any historical space to think of Hindu–Muslim unity in these critical times. On the contrary, his formulations validate the core Hindutva claims. The destruction of Babri Masjid becomes valid because it symbolizes Hindu cultural awakening. The attacks on Sufi shrines get legitimacy because these Sufis were responsible for the cultural subjugation of Hindus. And finally, the Citizenship Amendment Act, 2019 finds an acceptability because it aims to provide protections to Pakistani and Bangladeshi Hindus!

Varma is very critical of the BJP for its aggressive anti-minority politics. He opposes the idea of the Hindu Rashtra and finds it counterproductive for Hindus.[15] However, the narrative of 'Hindu pride' he produces in this book justifies a Hindu nation. Varma is completely silent on this apparent contradiction in his argument. He wants us to believe that Hindu civilization survives because it is based on a 'Hindu-Satya'—an eternal truth that seems to constitute Hinduness in its entirety. This Hindu-Satya, nevertheless, becomes meaningful only when it is pitted against Muslims. It seems Varma's quest for Hindu pride eventually transforms into 'Hindu prejudice'.

It is clear that the 'Hindutva versus Hinduism' debate is actually a reflection of what may be liberal intellectual laziness. It is too late, too little! It is too late because Hindutva has been an established idiom of Indian politics for over two decades.

The non-BJP parties did not do anything to engage with Hinduism during this crucial period of time. They adhered to a highly vague and politically disastrous form of secularism. It is also too little because Sangh Parivar has spent considerable intellectual energy supported by conscious political moves to offer a completely different imagination of Hindutva. The liberals still rely on the old Savarkar–Golwalkar thesis as if nothing has changed in the last three decades.

The failure of the non-BJP parties in interpreting the changing meanings of Hindutva and its emergence as a political hegemony must not be seen through the prism of their perceived victimhood. They were in power for a long time. In a way, a conducive environment for the gradual and sustained spread of Hindu essentialism was created during the time of the UPA regime. In fact, the non-BJP parties did not engage with the changing realities and continued to uphold their old, outdated, evasive, ideological templates.

The Congress gave up the economic imagination of Nehru while defending his secularism. Fractions of Janata Dal ignored the social philosophy of Lohia and JP while upholding the banner of social justice. The Bahujan Samaj Party (BSP) took a complete U-turn in celebrating caste-based electoral engineering in the name of Ambedkarism. And the Communists lost interest in the class question while adhering to Marxism. In this context, 'secularism' and 'inclusion' perhaps were the only ready-to-use phrases that could provide an ideological justification for their political manoeuvring against the BJP-led Sangh Parivar. The electoral success of the BJP exposed the limitations of this political consensus.

The non-BJP parties have been clueless about Hindutva since 2014. Their ideological templates are out-of-date, and they do not have the intellectual capabilities to offer any fresh set of political ideas. This is precisely the reason why author–politicians

like Shashi Tharoor, and Pavan K. Varma are taking refuge in
the Hinduism-Hindutva debate. They want us to believe that
the collective aspirations of Indian people are always determined
by their religious beliefs. Hence, the 'right' kind of Hinduism is
sufficient to counter Hindutva politics.

III

New India and the scientific history

The Hinduism versus Hindutva debate also underlines a
strange obsession with history. This became very clear when
it was proposed that the National Archives of India (NAI)'s
Annexe building would be removed as per the requirements of
the Central Vista project.[16] It was natural for any professional
historian to feel concerned about the fate of valuable historical
documents, which are preserved in that building. As a
professional researcher, I was also apprehensive about this move.

However, I find the overtly political diagnosis offered by
a section of fellow historians in this case problematic.[17] There
was an argument that the restructuring of NAI was a strategic
move that aimed to dismantle the apparatus of 'evidence-based'
history in favour of 'myth-based' politics of nationalism. In my
view, this claim is not entirely invalid in the present context.
Yet, there is a serious problem with this kind of reductionist
approach. It stems from the old secular history /communal
politics binary that emerged in the early 1990s. *Babri Masjid
or Ram's Birthplace?: The Historians' Report to the Indian Nation*
(1991) is a good example of this approach.[18] This report aimed
at refuting the 'mythical claims' made by the VHP by evoking
legitimate historical-archaeological sources. It created the
impression that historians, like scientists, can produce the final
truth of the past.

This kind of historical objectivity was celebrated in the 1990s when secularism was the dominant idiom of Indian politics. However, the situation has changed completely. The political class, including the non-BJP parties, are not interested in principle-based secular politics. They do not wish to hurt Hindu 'emotions'. Even the nature of legal reasoning has also changed in a significant way. The Supreme Court did not recognize the *Historians' Report* as an objective/factual/evidence-based source. It was seen merely as an opinion in the Ayodhya title suit.[19]

Let us look at the placing of history in the Hindutva framework. It is true that contemporary Hindutva politics has posed a serious challenge to all forms of critical thinking and knowledge production. A new imagination of India's past is proposed that not merely rejects the secular version of Indian history, but also offers a completely different meaning of historical evidence and sources. According to Narendra Modi:

> . . . India's history is not what we study before examinations
> . . . Historians could not see how the society . . . reacted . . .
> As a result . . . many things of the history were left behind
> . . . the soul of any land is represented by the feelings of the
> people there . . . Political and military power is temporary,
> but the public sentiments expressed through art and culture
> are permanent. Thus, preserving our rich history . . . is very
> important for . . . every Indian.[20]

Evidence-based history is contrasted with the feelings, emotions and sentiments of people living in a geographically marked territory. Belief is given priority over evidence/source simply to reassert Hindu victimhood. This is precisely the line of reasoning and Hindutva politics followed in the Babri Masjid case.

It does not mean that this Hindutva is not interested in cultivating evidence-based arguments. Quite astonishingly, the pro-Hindutva intellectuals assert that the sources/evidence must be seen as hardcore scientific facts.[21] The purpose of history, according to them, is to offer an objective, value-free account of the past. This scientific orientation goes well with the belief-based formulations in an interesting way.

There have been various attempts in recent years to write alternative histories from the Hindutva-oriented point of view. However, these histories are not presented as any kind of authoritative historical account. The primary function of these narratives is simply to address a different kind of 'fact-lovers' or the 'neutral' English-speaking middle-class public.[22] One finds an interesting division of labour here. The construction of an aggressive emotion-based Hindutva past is meant for wider public consumption simply to nurture what is jokingly called the 'WhatsApp University'. Whereas the so-called neutral 'scientific-objective' histories are written to produce a backup—a justificatory argument in favour of Hindutva so as to discredit the idea of critical questioning.

Hindutva's opponents fail to understand the operative mechanism of Hindutva history. They envisage Hindutva's project entirely as an irrational, ahistorical and even unscientific exercise. We are told that historical records are self-explanatory; hence the destruction and/or relocation of the National Archives sources would mean the destruction of historical knowledge and that the Nehruvian project of history is the most objective evidence-based version of India's past on these grounds to refute Hindutva.

This liberal critique is problematic. Historical documents do not speak for themselves. They become 'sources' only when a framework of history is provided. Nehru was very clear about it. In 1949, when the question of an authoritative and comprehensive history of the freedom movement arose, he wrote:

Everything depends on the individual or individuals who will be put in charge of this work . . . This requires two qualities at least. One is an emotional and intellectual appreciation of what has taken place and the other is high literary ability . . . . it seems to me that the first step is to collect material.[23]

He further wrote to Maulana Azad:

I do not want second rate or shoddy work to commemorate our great struggle. Nor do I want a panegyric or a mere record of events. The critical faculty has to be exercised and things seen in perspective . . . it means a survey of all aspect of national activity during the past two generations and more especially during the last thirty years. That collection would become the nucleus of a national museum.'[24]

It is clear here that Nehru, unlike many Nehruvians, was not obsessed with sources. For him, historical imagination was more important than the availability of sources. That might be the reason why he was able to write *The Discovery of India* during his imprisonment at the Ahmednagar Fort.[25]

The liberal critique of Hindutva history suffers from a strange victimhood syndrome. Its intellectual laziness does not allow it to respond to Hindutva with a refined and constructive imagination of India's inclusive past. They always take refuge in old ideas of India proposed by Nehru, Gandhi and Ambedkar almost seventy years ago to counter Hindutva's New India.

IV

Political past(s) and academic histories

The institutional autonomy of academic bodies such as the National Archives is very significant. The historical records must be protected transparently to maintain the credibility of professional academic research. However, we need to differentiate between professional history and politically charged popular imaginations of the past. The domain of professional history—archives, universities, professional academic bodies, and research institutes—is governed differently. It follows rigorous procedures to produce historical arguments.

The past that is constructed in the realm of politics is not always contingent upon the protocol of professional history writing. This past is constructed through legends, myths, stories and a few symbols to justify certain political acts. This emotion-based past is never presented as history. Instead, it is evoked as a collective belief. The Ayodhya episode is the best example of this trajectory. How shall we respond to it? Shall we get out of the realm of academic history to refute this emotion-based past?

The Ayodhya issue actually suggests that the emotion-based past must be responded to at three different levels. First of all, it needs to be studied purely on historical grounds by following the established protocol of professional historical research. The myths and beliefs should be contrasted with historical sources and the veracity of symbols ought to be evaluated.

This historical evaluation is further interrogated by asking what political theorist Sudipta Kaviraj calls the 'second order political questions'.[26] At this stage, one must study the operative mechanism of an emotion-based past: how is it transformed into a political programme? What kind of resources (propaganda materials, including fake news) are used to legitimize it? What kind of political vocabulary does it produce? How does it reconfigure competitive politics, especially its electoral version?

However, the third level is very crucial and demanding. The public intellectuals and political elites, particularly those who are critical of the emotion-based past, are expected to elaborate the scope of serious historical explanation and political analysis. They have to configure political arguments in straightforward language.

Academics, in my view, have worked very hard to question the limitation of the Hindutva imagination of the Indian past and its operative mechanism. There is considerable academic literature on it.[27] However, this professional academic critique of Hindutva has not yet found an argumentative political language. This shows the failure of liberal public intellectuals and non-BJP political elites. They envisage an instrumental relationship between academic arguments and popular politics.

V

Towards an alternative imagination of the Muslim past

Let us go back to the historical project of Hindutva's opponents. Our discussion shows that they have failed to evolve an effective mode to accommodate Muslims in their proposed version of Hinduism. Their elusive search for a counter-narrative to Hindutva is not fully comfortable with Muslim identity. Muslims are seen as a 'victim community' to reject Hindutva-driven majoritarianism and anti-Muslim violence. At the same time, there is a conspicuous silence on a few critical issues such as the desecration of Hindu temples by Muslim rulers, the class and caste divide among Muslims and the nature of Muslim patriarchy. This intellectual evasiveness produces a weak, unconvincing, superficial and highly essentialist imagination of Muslim presence. It seems that Hindutva's critique also envisages Muslims as a 'problem category'.

In my view, an alternative imagination of Muslim presence in today's India is possible that might help us to reconstruct an engaging narrative. Two possible avenues may be identified that provide us with a few clues for such an intellectual exploration:

(a) Liberating Muslims from the burden of ruler-centric elite Muslim history, and (b) evolving a moral-political justification for Muslim citizenship.

Two important facts must be highlighted. First, Muslim communities were not the beneficiaries of Muslim rule. Except for the ruling classes, Muslims have always been poor and marginalized. This historical realization explains why there has always been a power structure among Muslim communities based on factors such as class, caste, gender, status and prestige. Secondly, Muslims did not follow only one kind of Islam. There were various Islam(s) that evolved through a slow and gradual process in accordance with local customs and beliefs. These slow changes do not usually attract historians, who are trained to rely only on conflicts to understand social change.

The subaltern status of common Muslims during medieval times, and the slow, gradual, peaceful and non-interfering presence of a highly localized Islam allow us to think of a de-historicized Muslim past. An argument can be made that the common Muslims, who practice a variety of Islam, are not at all responsible for the acts of Muslim rulers. It is certainly possible that Muslim rulers demolished Hindu temples in the medieval period. This very act symbolizes a history of conflict, the political zeal of Muslim kings, and an apparent 'misuse' of Islam that has nothing to do with the everyday life of Muslims of that time.

A highly diversified Islamic faith system practised by Muslims in today's India actually represents a 'living Muslim heritage'—a heritage that does not need any legitimacy from the history of a 'royal Muslim past'. Hindu women with young children, who gather outside mosques for *dua*, especially after the evening namaz (Maghrib) are one such symbol of the significance of this shared Islamic legacy.

Figure 3.1: A Hindu woman with her child at the doorstep
of a mosque in east Delhi. The Imam is expected to make
a prayer for the child.

(Photo: Author)

Similarly, letters written by individual Muslims and Hindus
addressing '*Peer Baba*' to solve individual problems at Delhi's
Kotla Ferozeshah also confirm that Hindutva politics does not
have the capacity to dismantle the faith of the people, especially
Hindus, in the everyday existence of Islam.

This brings us to the second possible avenue: the idea
of Muslim citizenship. The advent of Hindutva politics in
the late 1980s forced the secular elite to recognize the legal–
constitutional framework as a viable mode to protect Muslims
as a constitutional minority. This ultimate submission to a
particular understanding of constitutionalism somehow has
created the impression that the Constitution of India has the

capacity to defend itself. Since Muslim citizenship is protected by this legal document, it is assumed that there is no need for any 'additional' political explanation. The CAA 2019 has actually proved that the Constitution is subject to multiple interpretations, including a Hindutva reading of it (as discussed in the second chapter of this book). Interestingly, the opponents of Hindutva as well as the Muslim intellectual–political elite are still suffering from a kind of intellectual laziness. They tend to view Muslim citizenship in purely legal terms.

Figure 3.2: Letters addressed to a jinn, Peer Baba by Hindu devotees seeking spiritual help at Delhi's Ferozeshah Kotla

(Source: Author)

This imagination of Muslim citizenship is problematic in two different ways. First, it has helped Hindutva politics to silently reduce the CAA–National Register of Citizens (NRC) issue to its conventional framework—'Hindu victimhood' versus 'Muslim appeasement'. Second, the inherent problems in the CAA itself are relegated to the margins. No one talks about the fact that CAA is actually an anti-Hindu law, which makes a migrant Hindu stateless for five years without any promise that he/she would eventually get Indian citizenship![28] Muslim citizenship is not entirely a legal phenomenon. Of course, the protection of the law is necessary for all minorities and deprived sections so as to assert the membership of the state. Yet, there is a possibility to rethink this question from the prism of actual politics. The nature of the anti-CAA protests clearly underlines this fact. Muslim communities enthusiastically participated in these agitations and sit-ins and strongly asserted their legal status as citizens of India. At the same time, they made a powerful moral argument in favour of their Indian identity.[29]

Politics, we must remember, constructs its version of past and future. Popular belief and everyday interactions of communities are political sources that could be utilized for refashioning a constructive imagination of Muslim presence and its place in India's past, present and future. There is an immense possibility to use this 'living archive'. However, it depends on political will and intellectual honesty.

Chapter 4

New India and the Muslim *Cultural*

I

The enigma called Muslim heritage

Our discussion on the Muslim past in the previous chapter can only become meaningful if it is examined in relation to the contemporary politics of Muslim heritage. It is clear that the aggressive Hindutva politics of identity has successfully redefined the historical presence of Muslim rule as a controversial period of Indian history. In this sense, Indian Muslim heritage—especially its architectural manifestations such as historic mosques, tombs, shrines etc. situated in different parts of the country—has become a highly disputed political entity. Hindutva politics defines it as a symbol of Hindu subjugation under the Islamic rule. Often, Hindu individuals and communities are mobilized to give up any possible association with Muslim-built heritage simply to reimagine their historical existence in pure Hindu terms. In a way, it has become a new political common sense shared by the entire political class.

The Hindutva politics of heritage has also posed a serious challenge to the Nehruvian liberals and the non-BJP parties. They take refuge in the age-old idea of composite nationalism to show the divisiveness of Hindutva politics. This important criticism of Hindutva, however, is not supported by any argumentative politics of secularism. Consequently, the non-BJP parties prefer to remain silent on the question of Muslim heritage, while a few self-declared liberals unnecessarily take recourse to redefining and re-examining controversial figures such as Aurangzeb.

In both cases, the Muslim communities are 'forced' to associate themselves with a few medieval Muslim rulers. Hindutva wants them to think of Qutub Minar or Taj Mahal as symbols of 'their' atrocities while a section of liberals celebrates everything associated with Mughals in the name of secularism and minority rights. To understand this reconfigured notion of political time, we have to look at how Muslim heritage is defined, demarcated, overlooked and even disregarded for obvious political purposes.

Historically speaking, the notion of 'Indian Muslim architectural heritage' was coined by colonial authors and archaeologists in the nineteenth century. Treating Indian historic buildings as authentic sources to write a factual history of India, the colonial scholars categorized the Indian buildings on a religious basis. The classifications of Indian history into 'Hindu-ancient', 'Muslim-medieval' and the 'British-modern' was the dominant framework in which monuments of each group had to be placed. As a result, a contested notion of Muslim architectural heritage emerged in the early twentieth century. This was exactly the time when the process of 'monumentalization'—the transformation of Indian historic buildings into legally protected monuments—began to take political shape.

Muslim heritage, in this sense, was 'contested' on two grounds. First, there was a historical argument. Colonial authors such as Thomas Maurice, who wrote the famous book, *Indian Antiquities*

(1794), recognized the desecration of Hindu temples by Muslim invaders as one of the determining forces for historical change in the Indian subcontinent.[1] This historical 'finding' transformed every historic building or site that had any connection with Indian Islam into a historically controversial entity.

The second related argument was archaeological in nature. The conservation of Indo-Islamic sites as 'protected monuments' by the colonial authority contradicted the stated objective of colonial archaeology, namely the 'search for the real authentic Hindu past'. For this reason, the Muslim heritage was to be protected in such a way that the possibility of excavating the Hindu past from the same site could remain an option.[2]

Hindutva politics, especially after the re-opening of the Babri Masjid for regular Hindu worship in 1986, selectively appropriated these colonial arguments. The 'search for real Hindu past' is identified as an unfinished project simply to produce anti-Muslim controversies on a regular basis. Hindutva groups only focus on those mosques, tombs and historic structures, which have a contentious communal past. They are not interested in undisputed, non-controversial sites such as old temples to enrich the archaeological map of India even from their own point of view.

Contemporary Hindutva problematizes the notion of Muslim heritage in three ways. First of all, there is a 'civilizational argument'. The temple-mosque controversies in Ayodhya, Varanasi and Mathura are revealing examples of this attitude. It is claimed that Muslim rulers destroyed sacred Hindu temples simply to establish the civilizational supremacy of Islam over Hinduism. Therefore, there is a need to reconvert these mosques into temples once again in order to recover the authentic Hindu civilization.[3]

Secondly, there is a 'class argument'. Hindutva's polemical position on a few famous historic buildings such as the

Taj Mahal, Jama Masjid and Qutub Minar represents a different-yet-strategic attitude. An imaginary dividing line between the artistic values associated with these buildings and the religious–social formation in medieval India is drawn. It is claimed that these buildings symbolize the creative aptitude of Indian artisans; hence, these aesthetic attributes must be appreciated. At the same time, we are told that the class structure of that society should also be kept in mind. After all, Muslims were the ruling elites, while Hindus/Indians were the subalterns in medieval times! The UP chief minister, Yogi Adityanath's comment on the Taj Mahal is a good example in this regard. He argued that the Taj Mahal 'was built by the blood and sweat of Indians' and hence its Indianness should be given more prominence.[4]

Finally, there is a highly vague and ambiguous Hindutva attitude towards Sufi shrines such as the Dargah of Khawaja Moinuddin Chishti in Ajmer or Nizamuddin Dargah in Delhi. It is worth noting that the Sufi tradition might also be seen as a kind of Indianization of Islam, something that goes well with the old Jan Sangh/RSS argument. The BJP has also proactively recognized the contribution of Sufis. The growing interest of the Sangh Parivar in Dara Shikoh underlines this fact.[5] However, one also finds a kind of unease with Sufism in the Hindutva discourse. The RSS's careful response to the debate on Sai Baba ('Sai Baba never claimed he is God; everybody free to choose whom to worship' was their statement) is a good example of this line of thinking.[6]

The opponents of Hindutva do not pay attention to this diversity of Hindutva politics. Their intellectual laziness does not allow them to recognize the inherent weakness of Hindutva's critique of Muslim heritage. Nehru's 'melting pot thesis' is still very relevant to offer a positive meaning to the contribution of different cultures, races, religions and civilizations in the Indian context. Hindutva politics cannot ignore the symbolic presence of the Taj Mahal as an Indo-Islamic building. Obviously, every Hindu of Agra is likely aware of the fact that the Taj has a functional mosque in it and that it is a Muslim structure. Yet, he/she does not hesitate to make a cultural claim on it. In other words, the contradiction between Muslim legacy and Indian tradition disappears when historic buildings and sites are envisaged as 'people's heritage'.

II

Gyanvapi: A new symbol of contested Muslim heritage

Let us examine the Gyanvapi mosque debate to elaborate on this point. The legal battle followed by the Archaeological Survey of India-led scientific survey of the mosque has transformed the Gyanvapi mosque complex into a disputed site. In 2021, the court accepted the legal claim made by five Hindu women for the 'restoration of Darshan, Pooja, Aarti, Bhog and performance of rituals at the principal seat of Asthan of Lord Adi Visheshwar and of Goddess Maa Shringar Gauri'.[7]

It is true that the Gyanvapi dispute is not entirely new. It has a long and violent history. Recent political developments, nevertheless, have given it a completely different direction. The conflict can no longer be described as a politically motivated mosque/temple dispute. It has now acquired a legitimate legal overtone, which is going to contribute significantly to the emerging political discourse. The conversion of the Gyanvapi mosque into a disputed site, broadly speaking, underlines three very important political aspects.

First of all, the status of the Gyanvapi mosque as a functional religious place of worship has an important political significance. Unlike Babri Masjid, which was a non-functional and almost abandoned structure, Gyanvapi is a living mosque. It is open for Muslim worshippers and they are allowed to use it for performing Namaz five times a day. This Muslim visibility did not pose any challenge to Hindu religious practices and rituals performed at various associated ghats around the Gyanvapi mosque complex in the past. Varanasi has always been a multi-religious city and it has never been possible to think of it in purely Hindu religious terms.

The recent developments, however, have transformed the Muslim presence in the city, especially around Ganga Ghats, into a problem category. The Kashi–Vishwanath Corridor, which aims to ensure easy movement of pilgrims and devotees between the ghats and the temple, has defined the urban landscape from an overtly Hindu perspective. There is no imagination of a functional mosque in this framework. There are designated routes to visit the temple, while there is no special arrangement for the Muslim worshippers. This new urban landscape has the potential to exclude Muslim presence in two ways. In a highly volatile anti-Muslim environment, it is very easy to envisage the existence of an Islamic place of worship inside a temple complex as a symbol of Hindu slavery and victimhood. At the same time, the history of Islamic iconoclasm, especially associated with Aurangzeb, also finds a hospitable space in this urban configuration. The proactive claim that contemporary Muslims celebrate the acts and deeds of Muslim rulers gets legitimacy in this schema.

The second aspect of Gyanvapi politics is inextricably linked to the Babri Masjid case, especially the legal closure of the dispute. Two kinds of arguments are made in this regard. On the one hand, the scope of local land disputes related to the places of worship is redefined in a broad civilizational framework. The inevitable clash between Hinduism and Islam as incompatible civilizations is evoked to establish a link between the Babri Masjid and the Gyanvapi mosque. It is alleged that Muslim rulers demolished Hindu temples primarily for religious purposes. In other words, Islamic religious practices are responsible for Hindu vulnerability.

There is also a 'site versus structure' argument. It has been claimed that the Gyanvapi dispute might be solved by evoking the formula adopted in the Ayodhya case. It is worth noting that the Supreme Court made a distinction between the site or the land and the built structure in the Ayodhya case. The site was given to Hindus to build a temple; while alternative space was given to Muslims to reconstruct a new mosque. It is suggested that a similar arrangement could be made in the Gyanvapi case as well.

This brings us to the third specific aspect of Gyanvapi politics. It is important to remember that the Gyanvapi dispute is not going to recreate any new secular-communal type political binary. Hindutva as a form of nationalism has already emerged as the hegemonic narrative of politics. Non-BJP political parties are not in a position to take up the issue of Gyanvapi mosque for any electoral adventure. They do not have the courage to take a principled position based on historical sensitivity and political pragmatism.

It certainly gives a political advantage to the BJP. Prime Minister Narendra Modi represents the Varanasi constituency in the Lok Sabha. He has taken a special interest in the redevelopment of the Kashi-Vishwanath corridor project. The Gyanvapi case, in this sense, fits well in this schema. The Gyanvapi dispute, it seems, is not going to be the central thematic concern for electoral politics in the near future. Likely, the opposition might not find any electoral potential in it. The BJP, on the other hand, will try to accommodate the legalization of the Gyanvapi issue in its broad Hindutva-centric development narrative. The legal proceedings, in this case, will contribute to existing political imaginations, arguments and claims.

III

Muslim heritage and the limits of law

The Places of Worship (Special Provisions) Act, 1991 has emerged as one of the most contested laws in recent times, especially concerning the Gyanvapi mosque dispute.[8] On the one hand, there is a positive reading of this Act, which reminds us that this law represents a national consensus regarding the existing religious character of all places of worship and their adequate legal protection. This reading relies heavily on Section 2 of this law, which says: ' . . . the religious character of a place of worship existing on 15 August 1947 shall continue to be the same as it existed on that day'.

There is also a negative reading of the 1991 Act. Hindutva groups claim that the existing religious character of a few religious places of worship, especially mosques, affects Hindu sensibilities. According to them, many of these historical mosques were constructed after demolishing Hindu temples by medieval Muslim rulers; hence, there is a need to reopen these cases for the sake of historical accountability.

The positive reading of the 1991 Act is definitely convincing. It calls upon Indian citizens to create a mature, tolerant and egalitarian society by accepting the true meanings of the *rule of law* and constitutionalism. No rational mind would disagree with this honest resolve. However, this well-intentioned proposal will only work if it is capable of responding to complicated and even provocative questions. In this sense, the claims made by Hindutva groups that medieval Muslim rulers desecrated Hindu temples and converted them into mosques cannot entirely be ruled out as politically motivated propaganda. After all, the desecration of religious places of worship was an acceptable political act in the medieval world.

These politically charged questions, interestingly, are always kept aside to assert the supremacy of the 1991 Act. This law is presented as a self-sustaining, morally superior, and legally sound mechanism to counter all kinds of divisive and/ or communal politics. This kind of legal reductionism, in my view, is politically counter-productive. There is a need to look at the political history that led to the enactment of the 1991 Act before making any sweeping generalizations.

The 1991 Act, we must remember, was an outcome of a particular political context. The re-discovery of the Babri Masjid dispute by Hindutva groups in the late 1980s encouraged them to refashion their position on Indo-Islamic heritage. The desecration of a Hindu temple was accepted as a workable political framework to legitimize the history of Hindu victimhood.

The Muslim political–religious elite responded to Hindutva politics very differently. They tried to expand the scope of their politics by evoking the debates on the religious characters of places of worship. This revisionist approach helped them to propose an intellectually refined and politically vibrant position on Babri Masjid.

In December 1986, the All-India Conference on the Babri Masjid was organized in Delhi. This Conference issued an overarching document—the 'Delhi Declaration'. This was the very first articulated Muslim statement on the Babri Masjid issue. The Declaration formally recognized Babri Masjid ' . . . as a national heritage and as a historical monument but, above all, as a place of Islamic worship'. The opening of the mosque for Hindu worship was not only described as a setback for Muslims but also as a violation of Article 25 of the Constitution.[9]

The Delhi Declaration also asserted two long-term objectives. First, it was demanded that all the historical mosques, protected by the Archaeological Survey of India (ASI) and the state archaeological departments should be opened for Muslims to offer Namaz inside them. Second, it was insisted that ' . . . in the interest of inter-communal harmony, . . . a Central Law [should be enacted] to guarantee the status of a place of worship and protecting it as it existed on 15 August 1947, against any claims thereto or any move to alter it.'

Muslim groups continued to highlight these demands in the period 1987–1991. Even during the time of state-sponsored negotiations between Vishwa Hindu Parishad (VHP), the Muslim groups (the Babri Masjid Movement Coordination Committee and the Babri Masjid Action Committee), the central law to protect the existing character of religious places of worship was discussed and debated thoroughly.

The Sangh Parivar was not in favour of a comprehensive law of this kind. For them, the Ayodhya dispute was a point for reference for nurturing a new kind of temple politics. L.K. Advani's Rath Yatra is a good example in this regard. The objective of this Yatra was to create a clear political link between the Ayodhya dispute and other contested places of worship.

In this highly volatile political environment, the 1991 Act was introduced as a 'compromise' to appease the radical Hindutva groups as well as the powerful Muslim elites.[10] By exempting the Ayodhya dispute from the purview of this law, the state recognized the Hindutva claim that Ayodhya was a matter of Hindu faith. At the same time, the demand made by Muslim elites that the religious character of all places of worship must be legally defined and protected was duly acknowledged.

It is important here to clarify that the 1991 Act does not cover all religious places of worship. The mosques, temples and other religious sites protected by the ASI as 'dead' historical monuments do not come under its purview. This provision is technically justifiable as there is a separate law (the Ancient Monuments and Archaeological Sites and Remains Act, 1958) for defining the religious character of historic sites.

However, this legal arrangement is politically complicated. The religious character of a historical monument is contingent upon the 'date of notification'. If no religious activity was going on the very date when a particular historic building/site was taken up by the ASI, it would have to be protected as a 'dead/secular' monument. Although it is legally not possible to reopen such sites for any religious activities, the ASI has permitted religious observance inside a few dead monuments in the recent past. In this sense, the 1991 Act opens up the possibilities for active politicization of the ASI. This is clearly evident now.

The 1991 Act, like any other legal document, can only become meaningful if it is supported by constructive, engaging and informed politics of inclusiveness. We must acknowledge the complexity of India's past in its entirety, including those uncomfortable historical facts that do not fit in the established narratives of secularism. At the same time, there is a need to assert the crucial distinction between spirituality and communal divisiveness. Spirituality, Gandhi reminds us, gives us hope to create a mature society; communal divisiveness, on the other hand, provokes us to take revenge. The politics of revenge cannot protect any religious places of worship even if it is protected by law.

IV

Muslim imaginations of Aurangzeb

Unlike Babri Masjid, the Gyanvapi mosque debate is more directly related to one of the most controversial figures of the Indian Muslim past—Aurangzeb. His religious policies are seen as a symbol of extreme Islamization and the demolition of a temple in Varanasi during his reign is described as a clear manifestation of his anti-Hindu attitude. It is even argued that

Aurangzeb is also responsible for Muslim separatist politics in colonial and postcolonial India. This popular representation of Aurangzeb encourages us to ask a few simple-yet-provocative questions: Do Indian Muslims recognize Aurangzeb as a symbol of their identity? Do they adhere to the political legacy of this last powerful Mughal? Is he really seen as an uncontested Islamic figure?

These simple questions are always ignored to reproduce two conflicting images of Aurangzeb: an Islamic tyrant, who demolished Hindu temples and imposed *Shariat*; and a devout and lenient Muslim, who even donated land to build Hindu places of worship! Interestingly, Aurangzeb has never been a Muslim hero. Muslim intellectuals, political elites and common Muslims find it difficult to embrace Aurangzeb as an Islamic icon. He is always seen as a problematic figure: an intolerant ruler, an untrustworthy son and brother, and an enemy of the universal message of Islam. In fact, Aurangzeb could not become a reliable symbol of Muslim politics in India.

Our public discourse, on the other hand, relies on a strong assumption that Muslims admire Aurangzeb as a respectable Islamic figure and that any attempt to defame him would eventually upset them. The demand to demolish the grave of Aurangzeb 'so that no separatists will come to bow on it' is a convincing manifestation of this belief.[11]

The secular reception of Aurangzeb is equally one-sided. A section of scholars wants to destroy the communal 'myths' to discover a 'tolerant and secular Aurangzeb'. There is a lot of literature on Aurangzeb that claims to produce a 'fact-based scientifically correct history' of seventeenth-century India to show the richness of the Mughal era.[12]

I find at least four Muslim positions that engage with the legacy of Aurangzeb and in a way take us beyond this Hindutva–secularism binary. The first position is sociological.

The so-called Muslim rule of Aurangzeb did not have any direct impact on the lives of Muslim communities. Although we do not have any reliable statistical information about the socio-economic status of Muslims in the seventeenth century, various historical studies show that the common Muslims, especially the Pasmanda groups, were poor, marginalized and socially backward. It is obvious for these subaltern Muslims to pay no attention to Aurangzeb's legacy, especially the political moves and imperial policies.

There is also a religious argument. We must remember that the decline of the Mughal empire after Aurangzeb's death was not seen entirely in political terms. The ulama class of the eighteenth century gave a powerful religious interpretation to explain the gradual deterioration of Muslim power. It was argued that the status and prestige of Muslims in India (as elsewhere) was weakened because Muslims had given up the true path of Islam.[13] Aurangzeb, interestingly, did not find any place in this quest for Islamic revival.

The second position is purely political. The Muslim League did not find Aurangzeb suitable for its politics of Muslim representation in colonial India. In the Amritsar session of the Muslim League in 1908, Barrister Syed Ali Imam made a very powerful argument on Indian Muslim history in his presidential address.

He said:

. . . The verdict of history is that in holding India under subjugation for centuries the Mohammedan held only her body and not her soul . . . The keen-sighted statesmanship of the great Akbar saw this and aimed at unification by conciliation, compromise and concession in religious, social and political directions. A long and tolerant reign of about fifty years proved the failure of this experiment . . . Aurangzeb . . . adopted desperate and hazardous method of religious

intolerance and forcible conversion. The experiment failed
again. Prejudices and practices of both the communities
sanctioned by the observance of ages defied cohesion.
Persuasion and persecution equally proved futile.[14]

Mohammad Iqbal, the Urdu-Persian poet, who is also
considered to be the philosophical founder of Pakistan, did
not deviate from this official version of the Muslim League.
Iqbal praised Aurangzeb for attempting to Islamize the entire
subcontinent. However, he also found his political method
'very rough' and counterproductive.[15]

The nationalist Muslims also had problems with the figure of
Aurangzeb. Maulana Azad's essay *Sarmad Shahid* (1910) offers
us an interesting criticism in this regard. Sarmad was a Sufi,
who advocated religious openness and opposed Aurangzeb for
imposing a rigid version of Islam. Azad gave a graphic account
of Sarmad's assassination. Criticizing the misuse of religion by
Aurangzeb, Azad writes:

> During any given period of Islamic history there are example
> of kings who made equal use of both the pain of the Qazi
> and the sword of the General in bleeding to death whosoever
> threatened their supremacy. Blood games were not only
> restricted to the Sufis and patriots, whoever dared to come
> close to the Mysteries of Reality and managed to read the
> intricacies of the Divine Sign was pounced upon by custodian
> of Fiqh. Sarmad was executed by the same sword . . . The
> myriad colors of Sarmad's blood seeped into Aurangzeb's life,
> and never again did he experience a single peaceful day. His
> dying days were spent in desolation away from home. But
> historians of the era were incapable of recording these facts.[16]

Finally, there is a positive position. There is significant
literature on him (mainly in Urdu written by Muslim authors)
that glamorizes his personality and his political vision.

Sadiq Hussain Sarhindi's Urdu novel *Alamgir* is a good example of this genre.[17] This literary representation of Aurangzeb heavily relies on a narrative of Hindu atrocities on Muslims during the reign of Shah Jahan. Aurangzeb, the pious Muslim and committed prince, we are told, had to take extreme measures to protect Muslim identity in the subcontinent. One finds a plea in these texts that the political and personal failures of Aurangzeb must be forgiven in the name of Islam.

These four Muslim positions offer very different interpretations of Aurangzeb's rule. Interestingly, they seem to agree that his personality does not have any symbolic capacity to create an everlasting impression. That might be one of the reasons why a majority of Muslim parents in India do not want to name their children after Aurangzeb.

V

The 'foreign' origin of Islam and India's Muslims

The Gyanvapi debate and its close association with Aurangzeb points towards a much bigger question—the foreign origin of Islam and the alien nature of Muslim heritage. In an October 2022 article, Pratap Bhanu Mehta has made a very persuasive argument in this regard. He argues that Hinduism should not be envisaged as a product of colonial knowledge.[18] Mehta recognizes the decisive role of British colonialism in producing a deeply problematic imagination of India's past. Yet, he does not subscribe to the view that Hinduism is an artificial entity that did not exist in the precolonial period. He claims that this kind of intellectual laziness is not capable of dealing with the serious challenges posed by the Hindutva project.

Mehta's thesis, in my view, cannot entirely be reduced to the 'Hinduism versus Hindutva' debate, which we discussed in the previous chapter. His revisionist approach encourages us to revisit a few critical and uncomfortable historical issues associated with Islam and Muslims. The foreign origin of Islam is a very relevant question in this regard. Hindutva politics evokes this issue to claim that there is an inevitable civilizational conflict between Islam and Hinduism. This conflict, the argument goes, can only be resolved if Muslim communities in India take responsibility for the acts and wrongdoings of medieval Muslim invaders. In other words, Muslims have to accept the supremacy of Hindutva's explanation of India's past, present and future.

Interestingly, the opponents of Hindutva employ a particular kind of historical reductionism to engage with such politically motivated formulations. The scope of the British's divide-and-rule politics is expanded to discard the claims made by colonial historians. At the same time, a neat, clean and harmonious imagination of medieval India is produced and sustained to reject Hindutva as an intellectually inferior and historically irrelevant political project. A revised version of this self-claimed secular imagination evolved in the 1990s, especially after the demolition of Babri Masjid. In order to refute the everyday demonization of Muslims, a section of historians began to celebrate Muslim rule and Muslim rulers.

This aggressive representation of Muslim rulers as secular figures contributed significantly to the Hindutva project. A new war of symbols began in the public domain even before the advent of Hindutva's political–electoral success. Rana Pratap, Shivaji and Padmini emerged as Hindu icons; while Akbar, Aurangzeb and Allauddin Khilji eventually became symbols of Muslim pride!

It is true that colonial history constructed a puzzling picture of India's past. The periodization of Indian history into ancient (Hindu/Buddhist-dominated), medieval (Muslim-dominated), and modern (British-dominated) has conditioned us to imagine India as a land of conflict and trouble. It is also true that the

Hindutva project has relied heavily on colonial historiography to shape its politics. Yet, one should not overstretch the role of colonial knowledge while engaging with contemporary concerns and anxieties.

Let us discuss the debate on the 'foreign origin' of Islam. According to Hindutva groups, Islam is an alien religion because it did not originate on Indian soil. For this reason, they claim, Muslims cannot follow the pure and unadulterated Indian culture and ethos. V.D. Savarkar's famous *punya bhumi* argument is often used to justify this assertion.[19]

We must note that this is actually a political question that revolves around a particular kind of postcolonial map-centred imagination of 'inside' and 'outside'. The official map of the Republic of India is seen as a permanent historical marker to define the tangible boundaries of the Hindu faith. This schema helps them to declare Islam and Christianity as alien religions.

Hindutva's obsession with boundaries and maps has its own limitations. A map becomes politically relevant when it is recognized as a cultural icon. This is only possible in a modern context where maps are circulated in a variety of ways for different purposes. It is easy for a twenty-first-century individual to visualize India's map as a reliable source to think of the internal and external borders of the nation and its faith communities.

However, this is not possible in a precolonial context. Individuals and communities did not have access to the map of the region, and for that matter, the state/empire they belonged to. They, of course, had a sense of 'boundary'; but it was qualitatively different from our modern perceptions. This was also true about their religion. They did not have printed copies of religious texts such as the Bhagavad Gita and the Quran. Similarly, the printed images of holy religious places or key religious figures were also not available to them. The religion was an amalgamation of a set of beliefs, rituals and practices. They were conscious of the distinctiveness of their faith and the operative status of caste relations. Yet, they did not have the resources to envisage Hinduism and Islam as world civilizations.

For instance, a Muslim individual of fifteenth-century Banaras might have been fully aware of the direction of Mecca. But for him/her, Mecca was certainly outside of his/her geographical location. However, there wasn't any possibility of treating this imagination of the 'outside' as a criterion to define his/her Islamic belief as an alien religion. Political philosopher Sudipta Kaviraj uses the expression 'fuzzy community' to explain this phenomenon. Colonialism affected the self-perception of fuzzy communities and eventually transformed them into 'enumerated communities' such as Hindus and Muslims.[20] This historical explanation exposes the inherent weaknesses in the Hindutva's conflict of civilizations thesis. Pratap Bhanu Mehta, however, does not want us to stop here. Instead, he pushes us to historicize the postcolonial political experiences more profoundly.

The existence of Pakistan on the map of South Asia, we must note, substantiates the old debate on Muslim separatism. The Hindutva claim that Muslims in India must always prove their patriotism and loyalty stems from this separatist imagination. The scope of this argument has been expanded in the last few years. Every aspect of Muslim social life is seen primarily as an anti-India/anti-Hindu act. Hindu–Muslim identities are very well defined as antagonistic entities and the principles of democratic accommodation are under threat.

However, there is another, and in a way, more creative way to look at the Hindutva critique. The decline of what is often called the Nehruvian consensus has paved the way to revisit some of the most fundamental questions of our political life.

The Muslim presence in India, in this sense, is perhaps the most important issue in this regard.

Hindutva groups have a very well-defined position on Muslim presence. The opponents of Hindutva, as we have argued in the previous sections, are clueless and confused. They have realized that addressing Muslims merely as a religious minority is not going to work in a Hindutva-dominated political environment. At the same time, they are not enthusiastic about offering any alternative possibility to establish inclusiveness as a political virtue.

Precisely for this reason, we need to assert a basic premise: Muslim heritage in contemporary India must be separated from the foreign origin of Islam thesis. Of course, Islam did not originate in India; yet it travelled to this land in a variety of ways as an idea when the notion of boundaries and borders were not imagined in the modern nation–state framework. The postcolonial Muslim political identity, on the other hand, originated in India as a rejection of European-style political system based on one nation-one religion-one culture. Muslim heritage, in this sense, is not merely related to those individuals and communities that recognize themselves as Muslims; instead, it is a defining feature of India's political existence as a democratic republic.

Chapter 5

New India and the Muslim *Religious*

I

Have they become more religious?

There is a popular belief that aggressive anti-Muslim Hindutva eventually makes Muslims more religious-oriented, ritualistic and visibly Islamic.[1] The correlation between Hindutva and Islamic religiosity is presented to us in a simple and straightforward manner. This simplified conclusion is slightly problematic because it is based on an assumption that Muslim religiosity can only be understood in relation to Hindutva. To go beyond this given interpretation, we have to look at changing patterns of Islamic religiosity, especially the 'location' of Islam in various 'survival strategies' adopted by Muslims.[2] More specifically, we must explore two broad questions: (a) what is the nature of anti-Muslim discourse in contemporary India? And (b) how does it impact Muslim religious orientation and practices?

I take a rather unconventional route to explore these broad questions. Instead of approaching Hindutva as a given and as an uncomplicated sociological phenomenon, I make a conscious attempt to trace the constitutive features of this discourse. Precisely for this reason, I find the term 'Islamophobia' rather unhelpful and vague. Although, it is true that events like 9/11 contributed significantly to the already existing prejudices and stereotypes associated with Muslim communities, the contemporary forms of anti-Muslim politics in India cannot merely be understood through the prism of the Western debate on Islamophobia.[3]

It is important here to clarify what I mean by 'Islamic religiosity'. Shahab Ahmed offers us a very valuable insight in this regard. He notes: 'A meaningful conceptualization of "Islam" as theoretical object and analytical category must come to terms with—indeed, be coherent with—the capaciousness, complexity, and, often, outright contradiction that obtains within the historical phenomenon that has proceeded from the human engagement with the idea and reality of Divine Communication to Muḥammad, the Messenger of God.'[4] I find this argument analytically useful. The interplay between the historical formation of a particular kind of Islam and the normative ideas contained in the religious–philosophical texts actually determine the nature of religious performances. Hence, the ways in which Indian Muslim communities express their faith in what they identify as Islam, become a possible vantage point to map out the character of those rituals and practices defined as Islamic. Islamic religiosity, hence, is not merely about the adherence to the five pillars of Islam (*shahada*, namaz [Salat], *roza* [*Soum*], *zakat*, *Haj*); instead, it accommodates those context–specific practices that transform Islam into a lived phenomenon.

II

Islamophobia or Muslim politicophobia?

Islamophobia, which simply means an intense dislike or fear of Islam/prejudice towards Muslims, is a Western notion. It aims to address the anxieties of the white-middle-class population in the US and Europe in the aftermath of the 'war against terror'.[5] Muslim identity, on the other hand, is an established 'problem category' in India. The involvement and participation of Muslim communities in political processes are often reduced to an imagined Muslim vote bank politics, while their social life is always seen as a symbol of backwardness.[6] The events of 9/11 intensified such apprehensions. Popular global phrases like Jihadi Islam, Islamic terrorism, Sharia Rule and so on offered new meanings to already established debates on Muslim separatism and Muslim isolation.

This interesting merger between the global anti-Islamism and anti-Muslim communalism specific to India led to a new political consensus, which may be called 'Muslim politicophobia'. Political parties adopted this refined mode to address Indian Muslims in the post-9/11 scenario not merely as a problematic religious minority but also as a part of a global Islamic ummah. Three defining features of this Muslim politicophobia are relevant to understanding the changing political attitudes towards Indian Muslims in the last two decades.

The slow and gradual transformation of Indian Muslim identity into an ultimate reference point for global Islamic terrorism is the first feature of Muslim politicophobia. The Islamic connection between India's Muslims and the Islamist/Jihadi organizations is evoked as the most legitimate template for making sense of violent events associated with Islam and Muslims. Two completely different official statements made by

Indian prime ministers in the aftermath of 9/11 are relevant to elaborate on this point.

In 2002, Atal Bihari Vajpayee argued stridently that Muslims 'want to spread their faith by resorting to terror and threats'. According to him:

> Wherever Muslims live, they don't like to live in co-existence with others, they don't like to mingle with others; and instead of propagating their ideas in a peaceful manner, they want to spread their faith by resorting to terror and threats. The world has become alert to this danger.[7]

Three years later Manmohan Singh made a very different argument. He took pride 'in the fact that, not one Indian Muslim has been found to have joined the Al-Qaeda'. Singh observed:

> I take pride in the fact that, although we have 150 million Muslims in our country as citizens, not one has been found to have joined the ranks of Al-Qaeda or participated in the activities of Taliban . . . this is because India is a functioning democracy. We are a secular state where all sections of the communities, regardless of religion, caste and creed, they may belong to . . . Being a democracy, being a secular democracy where all religions are free to practice their respective faiths without fear, without favour. I think that's something which has prevented that sort of eventuality.[8]

Although these statements offer us two opposite conclusions, the manner in which Muslim identity is linked to global terrorism clearly underlines the fact that Muslim presence in India is always seen as an imprint of global Islam.

The situation in Afghanistan wherein the Taliban came back to power in 2021 is a good example of how Muslim politicophobia functions in public discussions. A section of the Indian media has tried to interpret this crisis by evoking a strange speculative fear. They worked hard to find evidence and connections to prove that Indian Muslims subscribe to the ideology of the Taliban.[9] There is a popular conception that India (read Hindus) must not rule out the possibility of an internal version of the Taliban or the Indian Taliban precisely because there is a sizeable Muslim population.

The fear of active Muslim political engagement (or even the lack of it) is the second feature of Muslim politicophobia. The renewed debate on the Muslim vote bank in the last three decades is a good example of it. Muslims are alleged to vote as a collective in favour of a particular party at the national level. In the post-Babri Masjid scenario, the scope of this argument has been expanded. It is now claimed that Muslims primarily take part in electoral politics to teach a lesson to the BJP.

The 2020 Bihar Assembly Election is an appropriate illustration to understand this feature of Muslim politicophobia. The Hyderabad-based party All India Majlis-e-Ittehadul Muslimeen (AIMIM) won five Muslim-dominated constituencies in the Seemanchal region. The success of AIMIM under the leadership of Asaduddin Owaisi was seen as an Islamic response to BJP's Hindutva. Even serious secular commenters and non-BJP parties called out Muslim voters for their communal–Islamized voting responses. No one bothered to look at the political context of the Seemanchal region where caste among Muslims played a significant role in AIMIM's victory on those five easts. The party's winning candidates came from the numerically dominant caste of their respective constituencies: 'Surjapuri Shaikh for Akhtarul Iman, Anzar Naeemi, and Izhar Asfi in Kishanganj and Purnia districts, and Kulhaiya for Shahnawaz Alam in Araria district'.[10]

The almost insignificant vote share of the party at the state level (1.24 per cent) was also neglected simply to substantiate the imagined fear of Islamic expansionism in Indian politics.

The third feature of Muslim politicophobia is related to the popular representation of Muslims as a politically conscious community or what I call 'Siyasi Muslims'. It is assumed that Muslims are fully conscious and informed of their collective right and hence they always take politically motivated decisions. This perception has found a different overtone in recent years. Every aspect of Muslim social life is seen through the prism of global Jihadi politics. Muslim population growth is interpreted as 'population Jihad' as if couples from the community plan their families primarily to outnumber Hindus. Muslim personal law is seen as a blueprint of Sharia-based Islamic rule in India. An impression is created that Sharia is the only hurdle between egalitarian Hinduism and the modernist ideal of the UCC. The anti-conversion laws (which are strangely addressed as freedom of religion laws as well) are also based on this fear that poor and illiterate Hindus are converted to expand the influence of Islam in India.

It would be completely wrong to reduce Muslim politicophobia to Hindutva politics. Although the BJP has always been a clear beneficiary of this political discourse, the role of non-BJP parties and groups cannot be ignored. These erstwhile secular parties as well as the Muslim political elite were instrumental in creating a conducive environment for Hindutva to appropriate Muslim politicophobia.

III

Religious discrimination and Muslim anxieties

Let us look at Muslim responses to Muslim politicophobia. The Pew Report, *Religion in India: Tolerance and Segregation* is again very relevant here.[11] The Report reveals that only 24 per cent of Muslims think that there is a lot of discrimination against them in India. This figure obviously destabilizes the commonsensical view.[12] Aggressive Hindutva politics supported by media-driven, anti-Muslim discourse has led to many violent episodes. In fact, the lynching of innocent Muslim individuals in the name of cow worship has been completely normalized. It is legitimate for any curious observer of Indian public life to suspect this figure. The Report, however, does not present this finding as a conclusive answer. It unpacks this aggregate Muslim response in relation to regional diversity. This region-wise assessment offers us a very different picture.

Around 35 per cent of Muslims in north India claim that they have faced religious discrimination in the last one year (which was 2019; see: Table 5.1). One finds a very similar Muslim response in the North-east. Thirty-one per cent of Muslims confirm that there is a lot of discrimination against them in this region. The Muslim response in the central and western parts of the country is rather unexpected. These regions experienced a lot of communal violence in the past. The communal situation has also deteriorated over the years. Yet, we do not find any overwhelmingly critical Muslim response in these states.

Table 5.1: Muslims on Religious Discrimination

Region	Muslim Response
North	35
Central	10
East	27
West	24
South	29
North-East	31
All India	24

Per cent of Indian Muslims who say there is a lot of discrimination against Muslims in India today

(Source: Pew Research Centre)

These findings, I suggest, underline three serious aspects of religious discrimination in contemporary India. First, violent anti-Muslim Hindutva politics is a north-centric phenomenon. Although various reflections of this politics can be found in other parts of the country, the Babri Masjid dispute, the Shah Bano episode, the love jihad campaign, and the aggressive cow protection movement provide a contextual specificity to violent Hindutva in the North. This might be the reason why a sizeable number of Muslims in north India feel that they face serious religious discrimination.[13] This may also be true about the east and the north-east regions. The rise of the BJP in Assam and Bengal and the recent CAA protests seem to influence Muslim opinion in the North-east.

Second, this regional variation also demonstrates a very serious fact of our public life. Anti-Muslim discourse has now been normalized. We must remember that lynching of innocent Muslims or attacks on mosques and other Muslim religious places of worship even during the time of the Covid-19 pandemic are the violent outcomes of a sustained multidimensional anti-Muslim narrative. This narrative has become a part of our everyday life. Making communal remarks about Muslim individuals in public and spreading hate on social media is no longer seen as unusual or abnormal. This widespread normalization of Muslim bashing also influences Muslim opinions and perceptions. This explains the nature of Muslim response to religious discrimination in central and western India. In my view, Muslims, especially in these regions, do not think that communal slurs like *katwa* (circumcised), *mulla/mulli, miya, Jihadi, Pakistani* can also be seen as 'religious discrimination'.

Third, the overall Muslim reaction to various facets of religious discrimination also points towards a failure of violent Hindu essentialism. The act of lynching and its wider dissemination through popular media (WhatsApp, Facebook, Twitter, YouTube) is guided by two related impulses. It aims to mobilize a community of anti-Muslim warriors (the lumpen elements!), in the name of Hindutva. At the same time, there is a wider objective to create terror and fear in the minds of Muslims. The Pew survey shows that violent Hindu politics has not yet succeeded in terrorizing the Muslim mind.[14] One finds a strong inclination among Muslims in different parts of the country to constructively engage with the political system.[15]

IV

Mapping Muslim religiosity

It is important to remember that Muslim religiosity in India—an expressed adherence to Islamic belief by Muslims and the performance of religious practices such as namaz and roza—is always seen as a settled issue. It is strongly believed that Muslims are more religious than other religious communities and every aspect of their social life, especially their political worldview, is determined by Islam. This highly rigid assumption is often used in two very different ways. In a negative sense, Muslim religiosity always comes as a destabilizing phenomenon. For a rigid secular mind, Muslim adherence to Islam is an obstacle that prevents them from embracing modernity. Hindutva groups envisage, on the other hand, Muslim religiosity as a serious threat to Hinduism. Muslim congregational prayers and Islamic emphasis on community feeling/brotherhood are always described as a communal strategy to weaken Hindu presence. The old

Hindutva slogan, '*garv se kaho hum Hindu hai* [Proudly say we are Hindus]' actually underlines this anxiety. There is also a positive interpretation of Muslim religiosity. Some people claim that the crisis of identity, especially the challenge posed by aggressive Hindutva in recent years, would eventually force Muslim communities to take refuge in the domain of spirituality. In other words, the Hindutva threat will make Muslims more Islamic and practising.

Interestingly, the contemporary Muslim imaginations of Islam and religious practices are very different from these given explanations. Various survey-based studies conducted by CSDS–Lokniti, the Pew Research in 2021 as well as recent ethnographic works on Muslim communities tell us that Muslim religiosity is not at all a static phenomenon.[16] Muslims, like other religious communities, practice religion in a number of different ways.[17]

The CSDS–Lokiniti's recently published report *Indian Youth: Aspiration and Vision for the Future* is very relevant to making sense of the nature of religious observance among Muslim youth in India.[18] It is found that a significant majority of Muslims offer prayer (namaz) on an almost regular basis (86 per cent; 45 per cent of respondents say that they offer namaz five times a day). This finding demonstrates that Namaz is one of the major recognizable elements of Islam in India. However, this overwhelming acceptance of Namaz must also be seen in a comparative manner. A similar study conducted by CSDS–Lokniti in 2016 gives us a different picture. Around 97 per cent of Muslims claimed at that time that they offered Namaz on a regular basis. This means that there has been a clear decline in the number of Muslim worshippers over five years (before 2023).[19]

Table 5.2: Muslim religiosity: A comparative picture

	Pray/ Offer Namaz	*Observing Fast*	*Read a religious book*
Men (All India)	*83*	*69*	57
Women (All India)	*91*	*85*	*61*
Muslim Men (All India)	86	84	65
Muslim Women (All India)	84	86	61

All figures are rounded off in per cent. N=6226

(Source: Indian Youth: Aspiration and Vision for the Future, 2021)

One finds a similar pattern in relation to the observance of fast (*Roza*) in the month of Ramzan. The 2021 report shows that around 85 per cent of young Muslim respondents affirmed that they observed fast regularly (Table 5.2). However, that was not the case in 2016 when 93 per cent of young Muslims confirmed that they observed fasts during Ramzan as a standard religious practice.

This comparative analysis, broadly speaking, shows that young Muslims are gradually moving away from religious practices. In fact, young Muslim women are relatively less religious than Muslim men. The caste divide among Muslims further complicates this picture. Table 3 shows that Muslim OBCs are more practising in terms of offering namaz and reciting the Quran at the all-India level. However, the Muslim General category in UP is slightly more practising than Muslim OBCs (Table 5.3).

Table 5.3: Nature of Muslim religiosity

	Pray/Offer Namaz (regularly and sometimes)	Observing Fast (regularly and sometimes)	Read a religious book (regularly and sometimes)
Muslim General	*65*	*49*	*38*
Muslim OBCs	*75*	*43*	*47*
Muslim General in UP	78	60	52
Muslim OBCs in UP	72	55	47

All figures are rounded off in per cent. N=959 (UP N=391)
(Source: CSDS–Data unit Indian Youth: Aspiration and Vision for the Future, 2021 Survey)

Table 5.4: Belief system

	Belief in Fate	Belief in Karma	Belief in Astrology
Hindu	73	77	49
Muslim	63	77	22
Christian	46	54	14
Sikh	59	62	17
General population	70	76	44

Figures in per cent
(Source: Pew Research Centre)

Let us examine these findings in relation to the wider socio–cultural trends among different religious groups. The Pew Survey 2021 again becomes very useful. It shows that acceptance of fate and karma is an important feature of contemporary religiosity (Table 5.4). A significant majority of respondents (70 per cent) claim that they believe in fate—the idea that the life events of an individual are largely predetermined. Hindus (73 per cent), Muslims (63 per cent) and Sikhs (59 per cent) strongly assert this view. This is also true about the belief in karma. An influential majority comprising Hindus (77 per cent) and Muslims (77 per cent) and strongly adhere to this karma-oriented worldview. The perception that 'people will reap the benefits of their good deeds, and pay the price for their bad deeds, often in this life or in the next life' seems to be the sense in which the term 'karma' is understood. This fate/karma-centric religiosity actually explains the proliferation of an entirely new religious culture in India. There is an elusive search for divine men/women, Babas and Fakirs in all religions. The survey tells us that around 44 per cent of Indians believe in astrology.

The centrality of religious performances and rituals is another feature of contemporary religion in India. The Pew study asked about three crucial performative aspects and their religious significance: religious ceremonies for birth, celebration of marriage and death rituals and processions. Table 5.5 shows that the vast majority of Indians claim that it is very important to have these ceremonies in cultural as well as religious sense.

Finally, ritualistic religiosity seems to transform every religious group into culturally restricted social entities (Table 5.5). This is certainly true about Hindus and Muslims. A clear majority of Hindus (72 per cent) feel that a person who eats beef cannot be a Hindu. This view is even higher than the percentages of Hindus who say a person cannot be Hindu if he/she does not believe in God (49 per cent), does not go to a temple (48 per cent) or does not perform prayers (48 per cent).

Table 5.5: Ritualistic religion

	Religious naming ceremony for sons or daughters in their family	A religious wedding ceremony for themselves or the children in their family	A religious cremation/ burial for their loved ones
Hindu	76	86	85
Muslim	65	83	92
Christian	79	82	86
Sikh	72	81	81
General population	75	85	86

Figures in per cent

(Source: Pew Research Centre)

Table 5.6: Supremacy of dietary restrictions

A person cannot be Hindu if . . .	A person cannot be Muslim if . . .
He/she eats beef (72 per cent)	He/she eats pork (77 per cent)
He/she does not believe in God (49 per cent),	He/she does not believe in God (60 per cent),
He/she does not go to a temple (48 per cent)	He/she does not attend mosque (61 per cent)

(Source: Pew Research Centre)

Muslims also give priority to dietary restrictions to offer a clear definition of Muslim identity. More than three-quarters of Muslims (77 per cent) think that a person cannot be Muslim if he/she eats pork. Like Hindus, the belief in the existence of God (60 per cent) and/or attending mosque (61 per cent) are considered relatively less important aspects of Muslim identity (Table 5.6).

There is an interesting correlation between the emerging forms of religiosity and issues such as pandemics, unemployment, economic exploitation corruption and the decline of political and legal institutions. Table 5.7 shows that Indian communities do recognize the impacts of economic and political issues on their lives. However, their religiosity takes them in a different direction.

Table 5.7: Real problems of India

	Unemployment	Corruption	Communal violence
Hindu	84	76	65
Muslim	86	77	65
Christian	83	80	64
Sikh	93	85	78
General population	84	76	65

Figures in per cent

(Source: Pew Research Centre)

The three features of contemporary religion—the centrality of fate and karma, overt ritualism and supremacy of cultural practices—point towards an interesting configuration. Factors such as fate/karma and astrology pave the way for a strange process of *individuation*. This belief system encourages an individual to think of their personal sufferings as an outcome of their previous acts and actions. The impacts of larger social, economic and political processes on groups and communities are relegated to margin, and everything is explained in a highly personalized manner.

The overt ritualism and supremacy of cultural practices, however, function differently. These features remind an individual that he/she belongs to a well-defined religious-cultural community. To assert his/her place in this communally marked social space, an individual has to follow the established values, practices, customs and rituals of his/her particular community. This religious framework does not allow an individual to question the internal boundaries of religion. In fact, there is no room for any discussion on the rational aspects of religious philosophies and moral principles. The conventional distinction between spirituality and dogma is replaced by a dogmatic conception of religion.

V

Two meanings of contemporary Islamic religiosity

On the basis of this discussion, I wish to make two broad observations. It is clear that Muslim religiosity is facing a serious internal crisis. The impact of twentieth-century Islamic religious reform movements, which actually defined the contours of the religious domain, is gradually declining. These movements are no longer capable of responding to the emerging social and cultural issues young Muslims often encounter. The gradual marginalization of the Tablighi Jamaat is a good example in this regard.

The Tablighi Jamaat was a Sunni religious reform movement that redefined the concept of *dawa* (invitation to

Islam) in a significant way. Jamaat gives tremendous emphasis to Namaz-centric religion to invite Muslims to embrace Islam in purely spiritual terms. This non-controversial notion of dawa became very attractive for traumatized Muslim communities, especially in post-Partition north India. The Tablighi Jamaat gradually became the most dominant form of Sunni religiosity in later decades.

Tablighi Jamaat, however, has been facing a serious internal debate. In order to propagate a non-controversial Namaz-centric religion, Jamaat leaders discourage discussions and deliberations even on strictly spiritual aspects. There is no space for new ideas and energies in Jamaat's religious worldview. In a way, it has begun to disintegrate as a religious reform movement. The decline of such established forms of Islamic religiosity, it seems, has begun to unsettle Muslim religious imaginations slowly and gradually.[20] They still offer namaz and observe roza to assert their Muslimness, yet there is an increasing disenchantment with these practices. A specific form of Islamic conservativism, it seems, is clearly established, that not only defines the social outlooks and cultural preferences of Muslims, but also determines the everyday meanings of religion and religiosity. The crucial dividing line between spirituality and superstition is gradually declining and Islam is being understood purely in ritualistic terms.

The second observation is about the complex Muslim responses to aggressive Hindutva. The CSDS–Lokniti survey shows that young Muslims remain apprehensive about the fate of communal harmony in the country. A significant number of respondents also claim that they have experienced discrimination among friends because of their religion. These everyday concerns, however, are not entirely interpreted through the prism of religion or religiosity. Muslim respondents seem to interpret the growing intolerance in the country as a political phenomenon, which is often used for electoral mobilization.

These two broad observations introduce us to the complexities of everyday life of Muslims. It appears that Muslims create a thin dividing line between an inner domain of spirituality and the outer domain of politics. The crisis of religiosity is placed in the inner domain simply to explore new moral and ethical possibilities within the framework of Islam. The aggressive Hindutva, on the other hand, is seen as an essential element of the outer political domain to work out various survival strategies in an overtly hostile anti-Muslim environment.

Chapter 6

New India and the Muslim *Liberals*

I

Who are liberal Muslims?

Any discussion on the liberal Muslims in contemporary India will remain meaningless if the term 'liberal Muslims' is not adequately analysed. Many creative individuals identify as Muslim—artistes, authors, academics and journalists—who take stands against illiberal tendencies and religious extremism as their moral duty. The significance of their moral courage and political standpoint cannot be underestimated. Yet, one must critically analyse the sociological location of these liberal Muslims to find out the exact nature of their growing marginalization in public life.

A clarification is necessary here. I too belong to this category of liberal Muslims—not by choice but by conviction. However, I am fully aware of my privileged location. I was educated in premier educational institutions such as Delhi University and SOAS, University of London; I work as a professor in one of the leading research institutes of the country; I mostly write in English, and I do not face any kind of communal discrimination in my everyday interactions. Unlike a common north Indian,

Urdu medium-educated Muslim person, it is relatively easier for me to assert my progressive belief. The interconnection between one's conviction and his/her status, thus, requires a careful and sensitive assessment. This chapter, I confess, is written in the form of self-criticism for having an honest public debate on the predicament of 'people like us'!

A few questions are relevant here. Who are the liberal Muslims? What is their sociological location especially in relation to the highly diversified and heterogeneous Muslim identity? What is the nature of the Hindutva challenge, which has destabilized the status and appropriateness of liberal Muslims in public life in recent years? What kind of modernity do liberal Muslims (or at least a particular section) adhere to? What are the required qualifications for being a 'good Muslim' in the Hindutva-dominated public discourse? And finally, how do Muslim liberals contribute to the production of Muslimness?

There are two popular meanings of the term liberal Muslims. A set of individuals, who adhere to certain liberal egalitarian values without giving up their cultural and/or religious identity as a Muslim are often described as liberal Muslims. These individuals stridently oppose religious fundamentalism of all kinds, patriarchal norms and caste-based exploitation to make a case for an inclusive, secular and democratic society.

The term liberal Muslims is also used very differently to underline a sense of victimhood. It is argued that these liberal individuals do not subscribe to the dominant values and religious perceptions. For this reason, they remain marginalized in their own community. This imaginary divide between 'common Muslims' and liberal Muslims produces an interesting social hierarchy: a few individuals emerge as enlightened thinkers, while a vast majority of Muslims are considered an inward-looking lot. In other words, liberal Muslims get transformed into what may be called a 'minority within a minority'.

The term liberal Muslims, as an acceptable public expression, emerged only in the 1990s. After the demolition of the Babri Masjid in 1992, a new political narrative of secular inclusiveness began to take shape. The political class, led by the Congress, embraced secularism as an achievable political objective to reject BJP's Hindutva as a communal threat. At the same time, the Indian state also started advocating open market-driven globalization as the most preferred form of economy. In this volatile context, 'liberalism' as a theory of statecraft made a decisive comeback. The category 'liberal Muslims' is actually a by-product of this India-specific, market-friendly liberalism.

It is worth noting that the category of liberal Muslims has always been fluid and open-ended. It includes the 'nationalist' Muslims of the Nehruvian era, the 'progressive' Muslims (who used to take pride in their Marxism before the 1990s), the 'socialist' Muslims (who claimed to admire Lohia and JP), the 'cultural' Muslims (who described themselves as atheist but celebrated their Muslim identity in cultural terms) and the 'secular' Muslims. This rather vague and indistinctive character of this category was politically viable. One had to just make a politically appropriate gesture in public life to get legitimacy as an acceptable liberal Muslim, especially during the time of UPA-I. The uncritical celebration of the Sachar Committee Report 2006, for example, was one of the required criteria in this regard.

II

The problem of 'outdated' modernity

Let us examine the idea of liberal Muslims from the point of view of what is called 'modern thinking and outlook'. The takeover of power by the Taliban regime in Afghanistan in 2021 is a good example in this regard. A section of the so-called Indian ulema celebrated on social media the victory of the Taliban and it led to a serious public debate on what is called the Muslim mind. As expected, a few known self-declared liberal Muslims became proactive. They not merely criticized those who supported the Taliban regime but, in a way, questioned the backward-looking attitude of Indian Muslim communities.

I find this given imagination of an elitist 'liberal Islam' to counter religious essentialism deeply problematic. The liberal Muslims (who claim to assert moderate Islam) as well as the self-assured cultural Muslims (who celebrate their atheism in public life) seem to reproduce an age-old, rigid, inflexible and elite discourse of Muslim intellectual backwardness.

They blame Muslim communities for their conservative worldview and ask them to embrace modernity and rationalism for a better future. The cultural, social, regional, linguistic and even religious diversity among Muslims is completely ignored in this schema to sustain an enduring conflict between 'ulema-led regressive Islam' and 'liberals-led modernity'.

Take, for instance, actor Naseeruddin Shah's viral video released in the aftermath of the Taliban takeover of Afghanistan.[1] He makes three claims in it. First, the 'celebration of the barbarians by some sections of Indian Muslims is no less dangerous'. Second, Muslims should ask themselves 'if they want a reformed, modern Islam (*jiddatpasandi* modernity), or live with the old barbarism (*vahishipan*) of the past few centuries'.

The third claim is very personal. Describing his adherence to a particular form of religiosity, Shah argues, 'I am an Indian Muslim and as Mirza Ghalib said years ago, my relationship with God is informal. I don't need political religion.'[2]

No rational mind would disagree with his first argument. The Taliban regime represents a clear threat to the very idea of religious tolerance and the mutual co-existence of different faith communities. One must unequivocally resist it. However, the problem arises with his second proposition.

Like a visionary, Shah asks Indian Muslims to take a clear position on Islam. Interestingly, this question is posed as an MCQ (multiple choice question) with only two options: reformed Islam (modernity) or religious extremism (barbarianism).

This is a wrong question. Modernity stands for a specific cultural context that does not necessarily produce progressive religious reforms. The Taliban, for instance, are a modern phenomenon that evokes an instrumentalist reading of Islam to justify their political existence. Shah, it seems, is guided by an outdated modernist assumption that Indian Islam needs reforms to face the challenges of the modern world. He is completely unaware of the fact that there is a strong Muslim middle class in India that does not find any contradiction between egalitarian Islamic principles and modern ideas. Even poor and marginalized Muslims do not get attracted towards radicalism of any kind. They do not need any ulema or reformer to give them a prefect recipe for an ideal, reformed, modern Islam.

I have argued in my book *Siyasi Muslims (2019)* that aggressive Hindutva has virtually failed to provoke Muslims for religious extremism. It simply means that Muslim communities practice modern Islam in a variety of ways. Hence, asking them to prove their modernity and take a position on religious barbarism is an insult to their collective existence.

Shah's self-obsession with his version of Islam as an ideal form is also questionable. Of course, everyone has his/her own way of relating to Allah. Ghalib, Shah or Maudoodi cannot intervene in this intrinsic relationship. At the same time, this formal–informal link between a believer and Allah cannot be seen entirely as an individual pursuit. Shah wants us to believe that public manifestation of faith, especially in political terms, would always be dangerous, communal and violent.

This claim is based on a deeply one-sided imagination of modern politics. CSDS–Lokniti surveys have shown that Muslim communities participate in democratic politics with great enthusiasm.[3] Their religious faith and its public manifestation do not become a hurdle in asserting their status as voters and citizens. Shah actually follows the rigid conception of nineteenth-century European secularism that envisages a strict dividing line between the religion of an individual and their participation in politics. This form of secularism, political theorist Rajeev Bhargava reminds us, goes against the distinctiveness of the Indian version of constitutional secularism. Indian Constitution recognizes the cultural values of the public manifestation of religion to establish the 'unity in diversity' principle.[4]

This brings me to another interesting notion, the 'cultural Muslims'. Former Rajya Sabha MP, film story writer and lyrist Javed Akhtar (who describes himself as an equal opportunity atheist) is a vocal representative of this community.[5] Akhtar employs a theory of comparison. He compares the Taliban with RSS/Hindutva.[6] He compares the Taliban's decision to impose a ban on working women with those who support the practice of Triple Talaq in India.[7] And he also compares Hindu extremism with Muslim fundamentalism in India.[8]

These provocative comparisons are certainly important. There is a remarkable similarity between Hindu essentialism and Muslim extremism. However, one cannot universalize these similarities. Media-driven Hindutva politics that demonizes every aspect of collective Muslim existence in India does not need Owaisi, Muslim Personal Law Board or Imam to flourish. It has its own anti-Muslim agenda. Akhtar's theory of comparison does not allow him to go beyond the dominant media-centric debates and discover the changing world of Indian communities.

It would be completely inappropriate to disregard the opinions and views of great artistes like Naseeruddin Shah and Javed Akhtar. They need not do 'research projects' before making any public statements. Their freedom of expression must always be respected. At the same time, they are expected to be more informed, flexible and open. The liberal Islam/cultural Muslim framework they propose must accommodate subaltern voices and everyday forms of Islam. Otherwise, it would always remain elitist and exclusionary.

We must remember that Muslim communities do not have any platform to express their views and assert their opinion. Hindutva politics, Muslim politicians, media, Ulema, liberal Muslims, cultural Muslims, researchers and political commentators make observations on their behalf and ask them to 'behave' in certain 'acceptable' ways.

III

Liberal Muslims versus the 'right kind of Muslims'

Hindu nationalism has always been critical of the idea of secularism. The Jan Sangh wanted India to be declared a *Dharma Rajya*. This conception was revised in the 1990s. Leaders L.K. Advani began to use the expression 'pseudo-secularism' to argue that the BJP's vision of cultural nationalism represents the 'real secularism of the Indian kind'.[9] The BJP's electoral success post-2014 has forced the political class to almost abandon the term 'secularism'. This political decline of secularism as an acceptable feature of Indian public life has posed a challenge to liberal Muslims at least in three related ways.

First, the conventional binary between liberal Muslims and religious/traditionalist Muslims has become completely insignificant. Hindutva politics relies on the assumption that Islam and Hinduism represent two different and historically conflicting worldviews and civilizational ethos. Hence, Hindus and Muslims are to be identified purely on a 'communal' basis.

There is no scope for liberal Islam, and for that matter, liberal Muslims in this framework.

Second, liberal Muslims' adherence to secularism and liberal values was thought to empower them to speak on behalf of all 'concerned citizens' irrespective of their class, region or religion. This liberal–progressive position goes against Hindutva's claims that Muslims do not/should not represent Hindu interests. The liberalism of liberal Muslims is seen as a kind of communal conspiracy to establish Muslim supremacy over Hindus.

Finally, and perhaps most importantly, liberal Muslims do not have any direct political patronage. They do not fit in the Hindutva-driven electoral schema of the BJP. It is, therefore, obvious for the party to ignore them completely. On the other hand, the non-BJP parties are also not showing any interest in the liberal Muslims' version of secularism. These parties fear that any direct reference to Muslims/secularism/minority rights etc. will affect Hindu sentiments.

This clear abandonment of liberal Muslims by the political class must also be seen in a wider perspective. In this post-ideological era, 'winnability' has become an unwritten norm of politics. Consequently, winning elections has become more important for a political party than protecting its stated ideological principles. This has been one of the crucial reasons behind the hostile and indifferent attitude of political parties towards the intellectual class in contemporary India.

It does not mean that there is no scope for middle-class, English-educated, urban elite Muslims in Hindutva-dominated public life in India. Zafar Islam, Mukhtar Abbas Naqvi, Shah Nawaz Husain, Shazia Ilmi, Najma Heptulla and Arif Mohammad Khan are some of the known Muslim faces associated with the BJP. These individuals do have a cultural capital of their own, which helps them to carve out a space for themselves. Like the Muslim leaders of the Congress, they also adhere to BJP's official line.

However, they do not want to be recognized as liberal Muslims for two obvious practical reasons. First, they have to abide by the party line.

Zafar Islam argues that Muslims must give up self-imposed isolation;[10] Najma Heptulla claims that Muslims should look at their own problems first;[11] and Shehzad Poonawala's enthusiastically asserts that India is no country for appeasement and victim card politics anymore stem from the Indianization thesis of the RSS.[12] In other words, these 'right kind of Muslims' have to take a given position: Islam must be 'nationalized' and Indian Muslims should be 'Indianized'.

Secondly, the Hindutva discourse does not allow these Muslims leaders to step out from the set boundaries and/or to have an independent moral position. They have to show their complete devotion to Hindutva discourse. The public debate on the Bilkis Bano case is a good example in this regard.

BJP's spokesperson Shazia Ilmi wrote a very moving piece when the rapists of Bilkis Bano, a victim of gangrape during the 2002 Gujarat riots, were released from jail. Ilmi criticized the Vishwa Hindu Parishad (VHP) for felicitating these convicts. In order to create a sense of balance, she underlined a crucial difference between VHP and the BJP. She wrote:

> The felicitation of the remitted convicts was by members of the VHP. To attribute this to the BJP is particularly strange given the intense acrimony between the Gujarat BJP and Prime Minister Narendra Modi on the one hand and the VHP on the other . . . VHP is, on record, carrying out a campaign of vilification and defamation against PM Modi . . . That this felicitation was depraved is undeniable but the question is what exactly did this have to do with the BJP, given the history of acrimony between the two organisations?[13]

Ilmi's thoughtful, and in a way, vigilant internal criticism was refuted by the VHP in an interesting manner. In a rejoinder, VHP's spokesperson Pravesh Kumar Choudhry criticized Ilmi for being a Lutyens' elite. He argues, ' . . . so-called "secular" people like Ilmi do not have compassion for Hindu agony. They belong to the cabal of pseudo-seculars—specialists in raising selective outrage.'[14] As expected, no one from the BJP defended Ilmi and eventually the controversy died down.

This example shows that Hindutva's 'right' kind of Muslims are not expected to behave like liberal Muslims. Their sphere of operation is restricted. The moment they try to break this established faultline, they will be reprimanded.

Ilmi's episode is also useful to understand the reshaping of the Muslim intellectual sphere in contemporary India. The decline of direct political patronage for liberal Muslims has forced them to rethink their own privileged position. Hasan Suroor's book *Who Killed Liberal Islam* is a good example of this internal intellectual self-criticism.[15] The Pasmanda critique of caste-based Ashraf hegemony and the emergence of Muslim women as an independent political stakeholder have also widened the scope of critical discussions on Muslim identity. This vibrant Muslim intellectual sphere, I argue, provides space for democratic deliberations, discussions, criticisms and even self-criticisms. The role of liberal Muslims in liberalizing Islamic intellectual debates in a Hindutva-dominated environment cannot be ignored.

IV

Production of 'Muslimness'

Let us examine another similar episode to elaborate on the scope of this discussion. A section of Indian Muslims, especially those who are proactive on social media, celebrated the success of Recep Tayyip Erdoğan in Turkey. A number of posts written on Facebook and X (formerly known as Twitter) described Erdogan as a great Muslim figure committed to the revival of true Islam. It is also claimed that his premiership is an indication that Islam will eventually gain its lost glory and ideological supremacy in the near future.

Obviously, we do not have any reliable data source to ascertain the exact number of these social media users. Their enthusiastic appreciation of Erdogan, thus, should not be exaggerated to make any definitive comment on the attitude and anxieties of Indian Muslim communities. Nevertheless, one must carefully examine this phenomenon to unpack a paradoxical emotion: why do a section of fairly educated Indian Muslims admire a majoritarian regime in Turkey, while opposing Hindutva-driven majoritarianism in India?

Three sets of explanations are often given to answer this question. The first claim is rather sympathetic. It is argued that Muslims are facing an unprecedented crisis of identity in contemporary India. As members of a threatened and helpless community, it is obvious that they will admire the success stories of global Islam. It gives them courage, solace and a sense of collective achievement. This line of reasoning relies heavily on the given story of Muslim victimhood in Hindutva-dominated India. It legitimizes the Muslim attraction for global Islam as a 'Muslim reaction'.

Interestingly, the supporters of this claim—a section of self-declared liberals and a few Muslim essentialists—completely ignore the fact that their arguments, in a way, validate Hindutva's 'action–reaction' theory. Hindutva groups justify anti-Muslim feelings (and even violent acts such as lynching of innocent Muslims) as a kind of natural Hindu 'reaction'. This action–reaction framework is used to produce 'competitive victimhood'—a moral claim to legitimize those collective actions and moves, which cannot entirely be acceptable on ethical grounds. The contention that global Islamic terrorism provokes Hindus and nurtures anti-Muslim feelings among them is a good example in this regard.

There is a critical explanation as well. It is suggested that the Turkish state is trying to create legitimacy for itself in the Islamic world. The historic association of the Indian Muslim community with Turkey goes back to the days of the Khilafat movement in Britannica says 1919–2024. The revival of neo-Ottomanism in contemporary Turkey is publicized to revive that connection. The Turkish state, hence, uses its outreach to Indian Muslim leaders to create a conducive environment and visible global Muslim support.[16] This is a persuasive argument which explains the actual working of the 'propaganda mechanism'. Yet, it fails to clarify the nature of Indian Muslim association with the wider Islamic ummah. The liking for Turkish majoritarianism stems from an emotional–ideological orientation, which is often ignored in serious political analysis.

Finally, there is a polemical claim. It is said that Muslims as a minority will always support democracy and constitutionalism for strategic reasons. However, the moment they become a majority, their attitude changes dramatically. As a majority, the argument goes, Muslims would always prefer to have authoritarian regimes and strict Sharia rules. In other words, there is something specific about Muslims that makes them strategic and calculative.

There is an intrinsic problem in this claim. Minorities—religious, cultural, linguistic and sexual—rely heavily on legal constitutional discourse. The very presence of effective minorities in a democratic polity ensures the sanctity of the rule of law and constitutionalism. It saves the polity from the possible threat of majoritarianism. This is not specific to Muslims or Islam. For instance, Hindu organizations in the UK (and other parts of the western world) adhere to their minority identity as members of Black, Minority and Ethnic (BME) communities. They support the established protective mechanism and ethnic rights. However, many individuals associated with these Hindu community organizations do not hesitate to support the internationally active right-wing Hindu groups.[17] The success of Hindutva in India is admired and celebrated. Does it mean that Hindus also behave strategically in different situations?

We have to go beyond these straightforward answers. Muslim admiration for Erdogan, and for that matter the wider Muslim world, has to be seen in relation to the sociological diversity of Indian Muslim communities. In the first chapter of this book, I have made a crucial difference between the 'substantive Muslimness' and the 'discourse Muslimness'. In my view, this distinction is very important here to understand complex Muslim responses to global Islamic figures and crucial events in the Muslim world. Substantive Muslimness, which is constituted at the bottom level of society in everyday life situations, accommodates different attributes of a person's identity—caste, language, class and region. The discourse of Muslimness, on the other hand, imposes a few established and given meanings to Muslim communities, converting them into a homogeneous religious entity. The amalgamation and overlapping of these two forms of Muslimness produce interesting configurations. The admiration for Turkish majoritarianism must be analysed in relation to this complex making of Muslim identity.

Let me simplify this point. The global Islamic community, the Muslim ummah, occupies an interesting space in the everyday universe of Indian Muslim communities. They are fully aware of the fact that Islam is the second-largest religion in the world. They also associate themselves with this fact and ultimately become a part of an 'imagined community' of global umma. The proliferation of 'sacred images' of the central Islamic religious places—Kaba in Mecca and the Prophet's Mosque in Medina—provide a set of believable evidence to common Muslims to get connected with global Islam in a variety of ways. In this sense, global Islam becomes one of the elements that form the substantive Muslimness at the local level.

This localization of global Islam, however, does not become a contested issue, until it is appropriated by the Muslim elite to refashion the 'discourse of Muslimness'. The Muslim communities are told that they are part of a global ummah and for that reason, they have to follow certain norms to celebrate this intrinsic association. In a way, an informal, two-layered apparatus is established.

Let us systematically unpack Indian Muslim admiration for Erdogan to understand the actual workings of this apparatus. It is clear that the support for Erdogan is primarily expressed on social media. In this sense, Facebook, Twitter and Instagram emerge as the site where an uncontested emotion for the global community of Muslims is transformed into a question of Islamic identity. The pro-active Muslim social media influencers start behaving like 'representatives' to speak on behalf of Muslims. The figure of Erdogan is linked to a particular kind of Islamic revivalism. The reconversion of Hagia Sophia into a proper mosque is recognized as an example of it. This social media-centric performance empowers these Muslim stakeholders to legitimize their existence as conscious agents.

The intentional appropriation of this social media discourse by a section of public commentators is the second level where almost insignificant comments/posts are further changed into a national concern for a public debate. At this level of involvement, the sphere of participants expands immensely.

Three ready-to-use arguments, as I have highlighted above, are good examples to show how social media discussions produce/reproduce endless public debates. The unease of a few serious public commentators with pro-Turkish posts by a tiny English-educated section of Muslims on social media highlights this trajectory.

The Salman Rushdie controversy is a good example to elaborate on this point. It is worth noting that for common Muslims in India, Salman Rushdie was an unknown figure. In fact, they were not even fully aware of the legal-religious status of Ayatollah Khomeini in Iran at that time. Rajiv Gandhi's proactive move to ban *Satanic Verses* suddenly changed everything. The Muslim religious elite took up this opportunity to assert their status as spokespersons of Islam. The progressive Muslims, on the other hand, took advantage of this debate to become acceptable future-oriented 'good Muslims'. Consequently, in two years, the *Satanic Verses* became a Muslim issue.

The moral of the story is simple: Muslims' admiration for the global Islamic community is an uncontested emotion; it only becomes a controversial question when Muslim identity is instrumentally defined in civilizational terms.

Chapter 7

New India and the Muslim *Social*

I

What is Pasmanda discourse?

The enthusiasm of the BJP to reach out to Pasmanda Muslims has certainly made the non-BJP parties highly uncomfortable. Although the BJP has not yet introduced any concrete policy framework to address the needs of the Pasmanda communities, the party has been successful in exposing the unclear and overtly ambiguous attitude of the Opposition on this issue. The BJP's appropriation of the Pasmanda question has also increased the unease of a section of the upper caste–upper class Muslim elite. They make a few normative arguments to underline the Pasmanda assertion.[1]

First of all, there is an old Muslim unity thesis that is evoked to explain BJP's Pasmanda politics. It is argued that the Sangh Parivar is interested in dividing Muslims into Shia and Sunni, Sufi and Deobandi/Wahabi, and the Ashraf and Pasmanda to destabilize Muslim unity. This line of reasoning relies heavily on the traditional Muslim politics of minority rights that does not have any space for discussing the internal fault lines among Muslims.

107

The second argument is a bit sympathetic. Acknowledging the marginalization of Pasmanda Muslims in a purely legal–administrative sense, a section of the Muslim political elite argues that the inclusion of these downtrodden communities in the established framework of affirmative action is justifiable. The BJP's Pasmanda rhetoric is seen as a kind of deviation from the real plight of Muslim poor and marginalized communities. This legalistic argument is often exaggerated to overshadow caste-based inequalities and derogatory practices such as untouchability.[2]

Finally, there is a radical assertion that the entire Muslim community is facing an unprecedented crisis of identity in contemporary India and, therefore, raising the Pasmanda issue at this point in time is not at all appropriate. It is claimed that Pasmanda Muslim discourse has been systematically nurtured by the Sangh Parivar to highlight the internal weaknesses of Indian Muslims. Hence, there is no difference between the RSS-supported Muslim Rashtriya Manch and the organizations working for the Pasmanda cause.

No one can deny the fact that the BJP's position on the Pasmanda issue is highly unclear and vague. The BJP leadership always claims that the party envisages caste-based reservation simply as a legal–constitutional tool to reform Hindu society. For this reason, the party opposes the inclusion of Dalit and Pasmanda Muslims in the Scheduled Caste category. The BJP's Pasmanda outreach, in this sense, might be seen as a strategy to pacify those Hindutva-sympathizers, who do not fully subscribe to the party's radical anti-Muslim rhetoric.

Two questions become crucial here. What is the relevance of the Pasmanda discourse in today's India, especially when the public discourse is completely communalized, and Hindus and Muslims have emerged as ultimate political identities? Should we treat the Pasmanda issue merely as an 'internal matter' of the

Muslim community and stop talking about it in the name of Muslim unity?

In order to answer these questions, we must highlight three crucial aspects of Pasmanda discourse: its capacity to explain the nature of Muslim sociological heterogeneity; its assertion for complete secularization of affirmative action framework in India; and finally, its adherence to the politics of social justice.

The term 'Pasmanda' was coined by Ali Anwar Ansari, the ex-MP and the leader of the Pasmanda Muslim Mahaz in his book, *Masawat ki Jung* (2023). Pasmanda refers to a group of people who lag or cannot maintain the pace or progress. In this sense, Pasmanda is a caste- and religion-neutral concept, which tries to accommodate various forms of social stratification in its fold.

It is worth noting here that there is a hierarchical structure of Muslim caste groups in India, especially in northern and western states. The foreign-origin Muslim groups, who preferred to call themselves *Ashrafs* (noble born), became the upper caste, while the converted communities, the *Ajlafs* (lowly) and *Arzals* (excluded), turned out to be the lower castes in this schema.[3]

The Pasmanda discourse makes a serious attempt to redefine this categorization. It questions the Ashraf hegemony by highlighting the fact that Islam is an egalitarian religion that does not permit caste division (and for that matter any form of social stratification). At the same time, the non-Ashraf communities are described as Pasmanda Muslims and Dalit Muslims respectively to assert their dignified social existence as Islamic communities. This conceptual reworking expands the scope of Pasmanda discourse and empowers it to accommodate those forms of social stratification which do not fit in the conventional Asharf–Ajlaf–Arzal framework.

This brings us to the question of secularization of affirmative action policies. Pasmanda groups problematize the communal nature of the Scheduled Caste (SC) category. As is well-known, Dalit Muslims and Dalit Christians are not entitled to get the SC reservation. Pasmanda intellectuals, especially Ali Anwar Ansari, make a threefold argument in this regard. It is demanded that the SC category needs to be completely secularized to include all Dalit communities including Muslims and Christians. At the same time, the need to increase the quota for SC reservation is also recognized to avoid probable internal contestation amongst disadvantaged groups. Finally, the demand for reservation in the private sector is reiterated by underlining the adverse impact that the privatization of the economy has had on Pasmanda artisan communities.[4]

The connection of Pasmanda political discourse with social justice and economic equality without deviating from constitutional secularism is rather exceptional. Pasmanda politics, in this sense, is still guided by the constitutional ideals of justice and equality. The popular slogan used by Pasmanda groups in their pamphlets and rallies: *Dalit Pichda Ek Saman, Hindu Ho Ya Musalman* (Dalits and backwards are the same, whether they are Hindu or Muslim) highlights the fact that secularism of equality and justice is politically achievable.

II

BJP's professionalism

The BJP's Pasmanda policy actually stems from the party's professional attitude and managerial approach. This 'politics of professionalism' is almost ignored in public debates and discussions. The ideology of Hindutva is often exaggerated as the guiding principle for the BJP's politics. As a result, the party's mobilizational strategies and electoral tactics are reduced to Hindutva rhetoric. An impression is created that the party has been following a well-defined mission to achieve, what is called 'cultural nationalism' in overtly Hindu terms.

It is true that the BJP has been committed to adhering to the ideology of Hindutva since its inception. However, it does not mean that the party leaders do not pay attention to those practical considerations that do not fit well in the Hindutva-driven framework of politics. In fact, many a time the party does not hesitate to deviate from its ideological premises to deal with emerging political realities. The BJP, in fact, has produced a workable equilibrium that maintains a balance between the party's ideology and context-specific moves. The BJP's Pasmanda outreach is an excellent example of this politics of professionalism.

The BJP's Pasmanda policy is based on an interesting consideration. The party focuses entirely on the question of social stratification among Muslims to highlight the plight of Pasmandas. On the other hand, however, it rejects the Pasmanda demand for SC status arguing that the purpose of reservation in India is primarily to reform Hinduism. This complicated, and in a way, conflicting response, actually stems from the BJP's politics of professionalism. Let us take an example to elaborate on this point.

A broad overview of the recent CSDS–Lokniti Surveys (NES 2014, and NES 2019) suggests that BJP voters could be divided into three segments. The first category of voters may be called the 'committed voters'. These voters constitute the core support base for the party and remain committed to its programme and policies in changing circumstances. The BJP has expanded the scope of this political constituency in the post-2014 period. The party relies on its Hindutva rhetoric to nurture the aspirations of this segment of voters.

The second kind of BJP voters could be described as 'party sympathizers'. These voters identify themselves with the party and make efforts to create a public discourse in its favour. Unlike the committed voters, this segment remains vigilant and always forces the party to have a holistic approach. The 'Sabka Saath Sabka Vikas' slogan is actually meant for this segment.

Finally, there are 'floating voters'. These voters tend to associate with the winning party/candidate at the constituency level. The BJP's managerial approach has helped the party to gain the support of this segment over the years. Narendra Modi's popularity has also been an important factor in this regard. This configuration of voters reminds us that BJP as a professional party cannot ignore the anxieties of party synthesizers and/or the floating supporters. The aggressive Hindutva-based anti-Muslim narrative cannot satisfy these segments, especially in a context when the Opposition is also getting active.

The BJP is fully aware of the fact that only eight to nine per cent of Muslims vote for it at the all-India level.[5] There is no evidence to prove that the party gets any significant Pasmanda Muslim support. At the same time, aggressive Hindutva politics has reached its saturation point. The party needed a positive social narrative for the 2024 campaign. The objective of the Pasmanda outreach, in this sense, is to demonstrate an inclusive character of the party, at least symbolically. This strategy will not only help the party to deal with the worries and concerns of its sympathizers but also open effective channels of communication with the most deprived section of Muslims.

III

Pasmanda question and the social stratification

Let us look at four broad questions to elaborate the scope of this discussion: What is the analytical significance of the established categories, Ashraf, Ajlaf and Arzal, in making sense of the nature of Muslim sociological diversity? What is the official status of Ashraf and Arzal categories in the realm of policy discourse? What is the Hindutva response to this sociological categorization of Indian Muslim communities? Is there any relationship between social stratification and Muslim electoral responses? This conceptual interrogation might help us in evaluating the emerging forms of Muslim politics, especially in north India.

Imtiaz Ahmad identifies two limitations of sociological researchers on Indian Muslim communities in the early 1970s. First, there is an adherence to rigid historicism. He finds a tendency to overemphasize historical facts and categories to understand contemporary Muslim societies. This historicism gives us the impression that Indian Muslim societies can only be understood as a historical residue of their Islamic past.

The enthusiasm for macro generalizations is the second problem in this regard. Ahmad finds an elusive search for a fixed, permanent and universally applicable model for explaining Muslim sociological diversity. This type of research remains unsympathetic to micro-level complexities.[6] This interesting critique points towards the rigid boundaries of conventional sociological thinking about Indian Muslims.

Ghaus Ansari's 1960s work on UP Muslims must be seen in this intellectual backdrop. Ansari offered a neatly defined framework to study the hierarchical structure of Muslim caste groups. The foreign-origin Muslim groups, who preferred to call themselves Ashrafs (noble born), became the upper caste, while the converted communities, the Ajlafs (lowly) and Arzals (excluded), turned out to be the lower castes in this schema. This sociological division is further substantiated by an equally persuasive claim that Islam is an egalitarian religion that does not permit caste division (and for that matter any form of social stratification); hence, the existence of caste among Muslims is an entirely India-specific phenomenon.[7] This 'egalitarian Islam versus Muslim casteism' configuration reminds us that social stratification among Muslims is an unintended byproduct of Hinduism.[8] The intellectual and political significance of this argument cannot be underestimated. However, the Ashraf–Ajlaf–Arzal division cannot be treated as the standard explanation of Muslim sociological heterogeneity.[9] Imtiaz Ahmad offers us a very valuable suggestion in this regard. He argues:

> . . . the conception of Muslim society as divided into two broad categories, 'ashraf' and 'ajlaf', is a gross over-simplification of the existing reality . . . the 'ashraf-ajlaf' dichotomy presents a convenient set of values to people, and people do fit themselves into this frame. But the real units of social stratification are the caste-analogues, and the day-to-day relationships between different individuals in any local community are determined by their membership of the caste-analogue rather than by the broad categories. In the study of Muslim social stratification, therefore, it is the caste-analogue which constitutes a more significant analytical unit.[10]

A recent study on the practice of untouchability among Muslim communities in UP clearly shows that Dalit Muslims are victims of this social evil.[11] A section of Dalit Muslim respondents affirms that they do not sit with upper-caste Muslims on religious occasions and/or community feasts. It is also found that Dalit Muslims are served food on different plates. On the basis of these findings, the report concludes that the 'practice of untouchability is not confined to Hindus . . . It spreads far and wide and perhaps no Indian religious community can escape it, including the Muslims'.[12] The authors, however, also make another very crucial observation. They note: 'One has to admit that when it comes to enforcing these social sanctions with zeal, upper-caste Muslims are no match to their Hindu counterparts.'[13] Although this overtly comparative assessment gives a very realistic picture of Muslim casteism, especially in north India, it does not tell us about the specific forms in which untouchability is practised by Muslim upper castes. What kind of arguments do they offer in defence of it? What are their notions of superiority? How do Dalit Muslims look at the idea of Muslim homogeneity in religious terms? These questions need to be addressed more directly to have a meaningful discussion on the exact nature of the internal configuration of Muslim societies.[14]

IV

Pasmanda question and the contemporary policy discourse

Let us now turn to policy discourse to unearth the official debates on Muslim social heterogeny. It is important to remember here that the Indian constitutional framework employs terms like minority, Scheduled Castes and Scheduled Tribes as secular–administrative categories. If a social group is culturally/religiously/linguistically distinct and is numerically inferior to other groups in a particular social context, it would be recognized as a minority. If a social group, on the other hand, has faced caste-based atrocities and/or has been a victim of the practice of untouchability, it would be included in the Scheduled Castes. Likewise, the indigenous communities or tribes are to be officially recognized as Scheduled Tribes.

This neat conceptualization of administrative categories poses a serious technical question from our point of view: is it possible to address the socio-economic backwardness of marginalized Muslim communities or groups in the established policy discourse on affirmative action? This question is important because the Constitution empowers the state to identify the backwardness of social groups so as to design appropriate policies and administrative measures.[15]

The rise of Hindutva politics has affected this policy discourse on Muslim backwardness in a significant way in recent years. The BJP government does not have any clear position on Muslim backwardness. The slogan 'Sabka Saath Sabka Vikas' is often invoked as a legitimate policy response to dealing with the questions of diversity and empowerment. The BJP has refused to address Muslims as a specific segment. The idea of Muslim appeasement has been radically redefined in such a way that even the so-called secular political parties, including the Congress, feel hesitant to talk about Muslim empowerment.[16] However, the official policy discourse on Muslim backwardness is a bit different from the political rhetoric of Hindutva. Let me cite an example to explain this point.

In an article published in 2023 in the official journal of the BJP, *Kamal Sandesh*, Gopal Krishna Agarwal, national spokesperson of the party, described the Sachar Committee Report (2006) as a symbol of Muslim vote bank politics. He writes:

> The UPA during 2004 to 2014 tried to create divisions in the Indian society to reap electoral gains. [It] . . . had constituted Sachar Committee for Muslims and was trying to make changes, which were unconstitutional. A fabricated narrative in the name of 'Saffron Terror' was developed by Congress government in order to consolidate Muslim votes.[17]

This response is not at all unanticipated. The BJP has always been critical of what it calls 'Muslim appeasement' and the constitution of an official commission by former prime minister

Manmohan Singh specifically for Muslims goes well with the party's rhetoric of vote bank politics. Yet, this observation is not entirely correct. Narendra Modi government's Ministry of Minority Affairs still recognizes the Sachar Report as an important 'source book' for its schemes. In 2023, the ministry submitted an 'action taken report' to both Houses of Parliament with regard to the implementation of the Sachar Report.[18] The fifteen-point programme introduced by Manmohan Singh for the welfare of minorities is still treated as a fundamental principle to deal with the exclusion of minorities in general and Muslims in particular.[19] The ministry's website also features a report that was commissioned by the Government of India in 2016 on the impact of these fifteen points on minority communities.[20]

Does it mean that the Modi-led BJP is also involved in Muslim vote-bank politics? These apparent contradictions actually point towards two basic questions. First, is it possible to read the Sachar Report as a political project? If yes, what is the nature of this politics, which primarily revolves around the issues of social justice, backwardness and under representation of Muslims?

The story of the Sachar Report has received a new twist in recent years. The Congress has completely disassociated itself from it. The party's manifestos for assembly elections post-2014 are virtually silent about the recommendations of the Sachar Report. The leaders of the party are now very careful about the use of the word Muslim. For instance, the Madhya Pradesh election manifesto 2017 (which is called *vachanpatr*) employs the term *alpsankhyak* (minorities) for addressing Muslims and clubs it with *pichra varg* (backward classes) in order to make a few general promises about their development in the state.

The Sachar Report, as it appears, can be described as a context-driven political project of the Congress, which has lost its symbolic electoral capability. The Congress does not want to rely on the narrative of Muslim victimhood because it might upset its own version of Hindutva. Two crucial political aspects may be traced behind these shifting positions of political parties. First, the constitution of the Sachar Commission helped the UPA government and the Congress elite to recreate and sustain 'Muslim' as a legitimate political category. The report was used by Congress to mobilize Muslims as beneficiaries (though they were nothing but the object of an academic analysis). For the Hindutva forces and the BJP, the Sachar Report was evidence of Muslim appeasement, which was to be employed to secure the Hindutva vote bank in 2014. Second, the Sachar Report has an official status. It is an authoritative official account of Muslim marginalization, which is deeply rooted in public policy discourse on social justice. It is a compulsion for the government to follow it through at the ministry level. The BJP uses this administrative obligation differently. Unlike the Congress, it does not celebrate the ministry of minority affairs. Instead, the BJP wants to retain the Sachar Report—primarily because it can always be used as evidence to justify Hindu-victimhood politics.

V

'Muslim Caste' and electoral politics

There is a simple and uncomplicated explanation of Muslim electoral responses, which seems to dominate our public discussions. We are told that BJP has decided to focus entirely on its Hindutva constituency, and it does not have any interest in Muslim votes. The other political parties, the argument goes, have also accepted the BJP's narrative. They allegedly hesitate to approach Muslims directly assuming that Muslims would eventually have to vote for them. The emergence of Asaduddin Owaisi-led All India Majlis-e-Ittehadul Muslimeen (AIMIM), in this context, is seen as an attempt to polarize Muslim votes. Although there is an element of truth in this broad explanation, there is a need to go beyond the Hindutva triumph/Muslim victimhood binary to understand the complex nature of Muslim electoral responses. The BJP's politics of professionalism, which we discussed in the previous sections, is an important point of departure in this regard.

Two sets of questions are relevant. First, how does the demonization of Muslim identity in public discourse in the last few years affect their voting behaviour? What have been the impacts of Hindutva politics on Muslim self-perceptions? Do they behave as a political community? Secondly, what are their political expectations as voters? Does declining numbers of elected Muslim MLAs affect their political enthusiasm? If yes, what are the Muslim imaginations of political representation?

Let us take the electoral politics of UP as a case study to situate these questions in the backdrop of the post-2014 political scenario. The Muzaffarnagar riots of 2013 were a watershed moment in this regard. The BJP used this Jat-Muslim conflict initially to justify the love jihad campaign in western UP. The party continued to emphasize this violent conflict in later years. This aggressive anti-Muslim Hindutva politics helped the party to construct a Hindutva constituency of voters in the state. This led to the impressive victory of the BJP in the 2017 assembly election. The Yogi Adityanath government did not deviate from this set agenda.

The Hindu polarization, however, does not affect Muslim voting behaviour. Although the Samajwadi Party emerged as the first choice for Muslim electorates in 2017, they did not vote as a vote bank. Even the BJP managed to get 9 per cent votes. The caste–biradari configurations, economic class and regional considerations also played a significant role in this highly diversified Muslim electoral response (Table 7.1 and Table 7.2).

Table 7.1: Caste-wise Muslim voting in the UP Assembly Election 2017

	Congress	BJP	BSP	SP
Muslim OBC	32	8	13	35
Muslim General	12	13	18	46
Total	20	9	19	41

All figures are in per cent

(Source: UP Assembly Election Study 2017 CSDS Data unit)

Table 7.2: Class-wise Muslim voting in the UP Assembly Election 2017

	Congress	BJP	BSP	SP
Poor Muslims	17	10	10	51
Lower class Muslims	19	7	19	42
Middle class Muslims	22	9	25	35
Upper class Muslims	22	12	17	39
Total	20	9	19	41

All figures are in per cent

(Source: UP Assembly Election Study 2017 CSDS Data unit)

One finds a very similar political attitude of Muslim voters in the 2019 general election in UP. Despite the fact that the SP-BSP-RLD formed an electoral alliance, the

Mahagathbandhan, against the BJP, the nature of Muslim voting did not change. The Mahagathbandhan received overwhelming Muslim support. Yet, Muslim voters did not hesitate to vote for other parties (Table 7.3 and Table 7.4), including the BJP.

Table 7.3: Caste-wise Muslim voting in UP—Lok Sabha Election 2019

	Congress	BJP	BSP*	SP*	RLD*
Muslim OBC	13	5	24	40	12
Muslim General	19	9	38	28	1
Total	15	8	31	34	7

*BSP–SP–RLD were part of the Grand Alliance (Mahagathbandhan), All figures are in percentage

(Source: NES 2019 CSDS Data unit)

Table 7.4: Class-wise Muslim voting in UP—Lok Sabha Election 2019

	Congress	BJP	BSP*	SP*	RLD*
Poor Muslim	14	9	32	31	3
Lower class Muslim	16	6	31	34	7
Middle class Muslim	11	11	24	34	15
Upper class Muslim	20	5	27	42	8
Total	15	8	31	34	7

*BSP–SP–RLD were part of the Grand Alliance (Mahagathbandhan), All figures are in percentage

(Source: NES 2019 CSDS Data unit)

These survey-based findings underline two very crucial points. First, the demonization of Muslim identity in UP has been completely normalized. It has become a part of Muslim everyday existence. Aggressive anti-Muslim campaigns by BJP leaders or the lukewarm response of Congress or SP do not affect the political sensibilities of a Muslim voter. As a result, they continue to vote on the basis of their contextual considerations. This strong realization that Hindutva is the most dominant narrative of Indian politics also works differently. The poor, marginalized, unemployed Muslims of UP do not expect much from the outcome of the elections. Instead, they take it as an opportunity to establish an effective channel of communication with the political establishment. In a way, participation in electoral politics is seen as a mode to work out various survival strategies in a local context.

The CSDS Lokniti–APU's three-round survey-based study, *Politics and Society between Elections,* is very relevant here to understand this point.[21] This comprehensive study tries to map out the popular meanings of elections in twenty-four states, including UP. Table 7.5 underlines a crucial finding of this report. It shows that Councillors/Sarpanches are the basic point of contact for people at the local level. This is also true for Muslim voters. They have to engage with the local power structure on a regular basis to get basic official/administrative work done. In a highly volatile political environment, it is natural for Muslim communities of UP to envisage elections as a particular kind of survival strategy.

This brings us to the second set of questions—the significance of Muslim political representation. The difference between the Muslim political elite and the Muslim voter is very significant. My work on UP assembly debates in the post-Muzaffarnagar riots (2013) period shows that Muslim MPs and MLAs actually follow the party line in legislative bodies. Reducing them to their religious identity is rather misleading.[22]

It does not, however, mean that the presence of Muslims in assemblies and the Parliament is unimportant.

Table 7.5: Political expectations of voters in India

	MP	MLA	Councillor/ Sarpanch	Government official	Local political leader	Religious leader
Hindu	2	8	38	9	11	1
Muslim	1	10	34	9	11	4
Christian	1	8	15	11	8	9
Sikh	0	10	69	5	4	0
*Total	2	8	36	9	10	2

*Figures in per cent. Combined figures based on all three rounds 2016–2019. *Includes other religions as well.*
(Q. If you ever have difficulty in getting important work done, whom will you first think of approach?)
(Source: CSDS–APU Study)

To understand the complexities of Muslim representation, we must closely look at Muslim perceptions and attitudes. The CSDS Lokniti–APU study offers us a complex picture. Significant numbers of Muslim respondents (46 per cent) argue that they find it easier to contact a Muslim leader to get any administrative work done (Table 7.6). On the other hand, a powerful segment of Muslims (41 per cent) assert that the religion of a politician does not bother them at all. It simply means that Muslim voters do acknowledge the significance of Muslim-elected leaders. Yet, they are fully aware of the fact that professional politicians (including Muslim politicians) actually follow the usual rules of the game.

Table 7.6: Does the religion of a leader matter?

	Leader from the same religion	Leader from different religions	Will not make any difference	Don't know
Hindu	47	6	37	10
Muslim	46	5	41	8
Christian	58	3	27	12
Sikh	39	5	51	6
*Total	48	6	37	10

*Figures in per cent. Combined figures based on all three rounds 2016–2019. *Includes other religions as well. Q: 'Suppose there are two leaders from the same political party and equally competent to get your work done. If one is from your religion while the other is from a different religion. Whom would you be willing to contact first?'*

(Source: CSDS–APU Study)

The presence of the AIMIM in UP must be seen in this background. Asaduddin Owaisi has certainly carved out a space for himself and his party in the media-dominated public discourse. His speeches and arguments do attract Muslims. However, it is difficult to make any conclusive generalization about the AIMIM. The SP, BJP, Congress and even BJP do have their committed Muslim voters at the constituency level, which they would likely retain. In such a scenario, one should not expect any radical change in the Muslim voting pattern. The Muslim community in UP, as we have seen, is not a homogeneous political entity and Muslim voters do not vote primarily to defeat Hindutva.

This brings us to the main argument of this chapter. Social stratification among Indian Muslims is always understood in terms of caste-based division of Muslim societies. This rather restricted application of social stratification as an analytical template is problematic. The economic mobility of social groups in a long span of time and the elite formation based on the changing socio-political status of a section of individuals are equally important sociological factors. These aspects, however, are not given sufficient intellectual attention. Even the caste among Muslims is presented to us as a sociological 'discovery' to reproduce the 'Muslim minority-Hindu majority framework'.[23] Ambedkar was probably the first and only political commentator of the 1940s who recognizes this dilemma. He argues:

> . . . the reason for the absence of the spirit of change in the Indian Musalman is to be sought in the peculiar position he occupies in India. He is placed in a social environment which is predominantly Hindu. That Hindu environment is always silently but surely encroaching upon him. He feels that it is de-musalmanizing him. As a protection against this gradual weaning away, he is led to insist on preserving everything that is Islamic without caring to examine whether it is helpful or harmful to his society.[24]

Indian Muslim identity, Ambedkar reminds us here, is always constituted in relation to the Hindu-dominated environment. In our context, this Hindu environment has found a concrete expression in the political language of Hindutva. The contemporary Muslim identity, hence, cannot be understood without a proper analysis of different forms of political Hindutva.[25] The CSDS surveys give us an important indication in this regard. It is found that Muslim respondents often prefer to identify themselves as Muslims at the first instance. They mention their specific *zat or* biradari (especially in UP and Bihar) only when they are asked to categorically state their social groups or caste. In order to avoid such confusion, we employ two broad categories, Muslim General or Muslim OBCs, to organize this self-reported data/information in an officially acceptable framework. Despite following these very careful procedures, we often fail to accommodate a section of Muslims into these neatly designed categories.[26] It simply means that Muslim self-perception is a complicated phenomenon. Muslims invoke their Islamic identity not merely in religious terms. They also envisage themselves as a caste-like group in order to adjust themselves to the wider Hindu-dominated caste-based environment. The social universe of Muslim communities, however, is governed by a different logic. They adhere to caste-based status hierarchies and even practice untouchability. The interplay between these two seemingly conflicting self-perceptions actually determines their political behaviour at the local level.

Chapter 8

New India and the Muslim *Political*

I

How to understand Muslim political attitude

There has always been a curiosity to know 'how Muslims think and behave in secular India'. The rise of the Modi-led BJP as the dominant force at the national level has transformed this sincere concern into political anxiety. The BJP's Hindutva politics revolves around the slogan of 'Sabka Saath, Sabka Vikas, Sabka Vishwas' claiming that there is no need to treat Muslims as a separate social entity. Although the party is making serious efforts to reach out to the Pasmanda Muslim communities, Muslim political participation is still posed as an unresolved question.

The opponents of BJP are equally puzzled. It is true that the non-BJP parties have opposed aggressive Hindutva, especially its violent anti-Muslim manifestations. Rahul Gandhi's Bharat Jodo Yatra, which was supported by civil society organizations and people's movements, was a serious attempt in this regard. Yet, there is certainly an unease among the non-BJP groups. Despite emphasizing communal brotherhood as a core political value, the opposition parties do not want to be called 'pro-Muslim'. The impression that Muslim political attitude can only be understood as an anti-BJP phenomenon seems to guide their political strategy.

Let us attempt to unpack the complexities associated with these popular beliefs. Terms like 'political participation' and 'electoral behaviour' are often used interchangeably to explain different formulations of Muslim political attitudes. Muslim participation as a positive feature is evoked to celebrate India's adherence to plurality, inclusiveness and democratic constitutionalism. It is argued that the active involvement of Muslims in democratic processes—mainly in electoral politics—demonstrates that India's minorities do not feel isolated and marginalized.[1] However, there is a negative imagination of Muslim political participation. Muslims are seen as a politically conscious community, which is supposed to be fully aware of its communal interests. Hence, they participate in politics to bargain with the state for the protection of their collective, communal and eventually separatist interests.[2]

These two conflicting interpretations of Muslims' engagement with politics, interestingly, rely on a strong assumption that Muslim political attitude has been homogeneous, consistent and static—and precisely for this reason—it should always be analysed in relation to larger questions of Indian politics such as the success of democracy[3] and/or the threat of separatism/communalism.[4] As a result, the Muslim political attitude emerges as an analytically uncomplicated and politically self-explanatory phenomenon.[5] I use the term 'Muslim political attitude' to describe the highly diversified and even conflicting opinions and values Muslim individuals/communities hold about contemporary political debates (such as nationalism and Hindutva), critical events (such as lynching and communal riots) and influential personalities (such as Narendra Modi, Amit Shah and Asaduddin Owaisi) that determine their political actions in different contexts. More precisely, I invoke two related formulations—'political participation as interaction' and 'political participation as instrumental action'—to map out the contours of Muslim political attitudes.[6]

Participation as 'interaction' is about how Muslims as citizens interact with other citizens and groups; respond to public debates; and assert their opinions, anxieties and criticisms. This notion of participation envisages Muslims as active political actors, who participate in political/public activities as citizens with or without adhering to their Islamic belief and/or constitutionally recognized status as a religious minority.[7]

Participation as 'instrumental' action, on the other hand, introduces us to a more formal form of political action. Muslims, like other social groups, take part in political processes, especially in elections, as stakeholders to secure certain material benefits. They behave like consumers/clients and respond to the welfare packages offered by the political parties.[8] The elections, in this schema, turn out to be the most visible arena of politics where Muslim participation could easily be identified. However, the interaction between Muslim communities and the state in different regional and local contexts and numerous 'survival strategies' evolved out of it also produce different forms of participation, which may legitimately be called 'instrumental action'.[9]

II

Participation as interaction: Protest

The success of the BJP in 2014 contributed significantly to the revival of aggressive anti-Muslim Hindutva politics. Hindutva groups and a section of the pro-BJP media initiated a new discourse of nationalism. Every aspect of the social and cultural

life of Muslims in India was transformed into an unresolvable
civilizational conflict between Hinduism and Islam. Issues such
as the cow protection movement, protection of Hindu girls
from love jihad, Muslim population growth, the Ram temple in
Ayodhya, and the ban on triple talaq/introduction of UCC were
the constitutive elements of this Hindutva-driven discourse of
nationalism. This aggressive propaganda led to a new kind of
violence against Muslims—lynching, molestation and even
rape.[10] Despite this hostile anti-Muslim attitude, Muslim
communities did not get involved in any anti-Hindutva counter-
mobilization. Religious organizations, Muslim pressure groups
and even Muslim political leaders (except for a few unknown
faces, who appear on primetime TV every night!) did not call
upon the Muslims to launch any mass protest.[11]

However, this was not the case with the CAA Bill
introduced in 2019. Unlike the Babri Masjid case and the
triple talaq law, which had already lost the political potential
to provoke Muslims, the CAA/NRC posed a direct challenge
to the political existence of Muslims as legitimate citizens and
Muslim communities reacted to it more sharply. There were a
number of protests throughout the country against the CAA/
NRC. Muslims actively participated in these protests. Although
this Muslim assertiveness did not get any concrete formal–
organizational shape, the violent and even brutal reaction of
the state towards Muslim activists in later months underlines
the political significance of these protests.[12] Three broad facets
of these protests are relevant to highlight a particular form of
Muslim political attitudes: participation as interaction.[13]

The non-party character of anti-CAA protests is the first
distinctive aspect of Muslim assertions against the CAA. The
Muslim campaigners, it seems, drew inspiration from grassroots
politics and people's movements (such as movements against
displacements, Dalit/Adivasi movements, and the farmers'

agitations and so on) in two significant ways. They identified the Constitution as a legitimate political source for asserting their citizenship status. The liberal values of the Constitution, especially the Preamble, were creatively interpreted to question the disruptive agenda of the government. At the same time, an attempt was made to represent the anti-CAA protest as a non-party political agitation. This conscious move helped the protestors to get rid of the 'BJP versus Congress' framework. It also allowed them to portray the anti-CAA protest as an inclusive movement for social change.[14]

The invocation of national symbols is the second aspect of the anti-CAA protests. The national anthem, the national flag and even the copy of the Constitution were not merely seen as intellectual resources. The Muslim protestors also used them as political symbols. It is worth noting that this creative reinterpretation of national symbols is a relatively new phenomenon in Indian politics. The anti-corruption movement of 2011 was the first major political event when the official national symbols were recognized as legitimate sources of political agitation. The Muslim protestors, however, expanded the scope of this symbolism. The photographs of Ambedkar and Gandhi were placed side by side along with the copy of the Constitution; religious texts—Bhagavat Geeta, the Quran, the Bible and the Guru Granth Sahib—were recited in order to assert the postcolonial *'sarv dharm sambhav'* tradition; *havans* were organized for communal harmony; and the national anthem was sung on the stairs of the historic Jama Masjid in Delhi. This creative re-articulation of symbolic nationalism takes us beyond the given imaginations of Muslim political identity. The Muslim communities, who are often treated as religiously inward-looking and politically untrustworthy, seem to reassert the point that their Muslimness is an inseparable part of their Indian identity.

The refined idea of political representation is the third aspect of Muslim assertiveness. The Muslim protestors were not led by any particular Muslim organization or individual. It is true that the Hyderabad-based AIMIM organized a number of protests against the CAA and the Muslim religious bodies such as the Jamiat-Ulama-e-Hind and Jamat-e-Islami Hind have been very critical of this law. However, these established Muslim organizations were not given any formal recognition. The Muslim protests, in this sense, redefined the idea of representation in two possible ways. First, it was asserted, in fact rather stridently, that political anxiety associated with the CAA and NRC should not necessarily be represented exclusively by Muslim politicians. The presence of Dalit leaders and Sikh religious leaders in the Muslim-dominated anti-CAA protests throughout the country demonstrated the fact that Muslim communities refused to make the CAA an exclusive Muslim issue. Secondly, and perhaps most importantly, Muslim women—who were always depicted as victims of Islamic patriarchy—led these protests. The active participation of ordinary Muslim women in sit-ins and demonstrations as well as their vocal critique of the citizenship law underlines a new form of Muslim self-representation—the idea that challenges the authority of Muslim leaders (primarily male) to speak on behalf of common Muslims.[15]

III

Participation as interaction: Perceptions

The Social and Political Barometer Survey 2023 conducted by CSDS-Lokniti is my second example to explain Muslim political attitudes in terms of 'interaction'.[16] The findings of this survey offer us a complex picture, in which Hindus and Muslims do not always emerge as conflicting identities.

More specifically, the Muslim response to Narendra Modi's leadership as the Prime Minister of the country for over a decade provides insights for a serious discussion on the Muslim–Modi connection.

Three questions are relevant from our point of view. First, how do Muslims relate to basic existential issues such as poverty, unemployment, price rise etc.? Do they think differently? Second, how do Muslims evaluate the performance of the BJP government? Does this assessment influence their voting pattern? Finally, what is the Muslim perception of Narendra Modi? What are the qualities of leadership they identify in him?

For the sake of clarity, let us look at the Muslim perceptions in comparison to Hindu responses. Table 8.1 shows that a majority of Muslims believe that their economic condition has remained the same in the last four years. We do not find any stark difference between Hindu and Muslim opinion on this question, though it is also true that a sizeable number of Muslims claim that their economic condition has deteriorated during this period.

Table 8.1: Economic condition

	Better	**Remained Same**	**Worse**
Hindus	36	42	2
Muslims	28	44	28
Overall public opinion	35	42	22

All figures are in percentages. Figures may not add up to 100 due to rounding off. The rest did not respond

(Source: CSDS–Lokniti Social and Political Barometer Survey 2023. N=7202)

Table 8.2 further explains this complex Muslim response. We again find a remarkable consistency in Hindu and

Muslim views. Muslims, like other religious groups, feel that unemployment, poverty and price rise are the biggest issues that the country is facing at the moment.

Table 8.2: The national challenges

| | Issues India is facing today . . . | | | | |
	Unemployment	Poverty	Price rise/ inflation	Corruption/ scam	Other issues
Hindus	29	22	18	5	23
Muslims	26	20	24	4	24
Overall public opinion	29	22	19	5	24

All figures are in per cent. Figures may not add up to 100 due to rounding off. The rest did not respond.

(Source: CSDS–Lokniti Social and Political Barometer Survey 2023. N=7202)

This raises the question of the capability of the government in dealing with present economic distress. The survey findings (Table 8.3) show that a vast majority of Indians think that the Modi government has failed to control the prices. Muslim respondents also subscribe to this view. In fact, they are more vocal in highlighting the economic failure of the government.

So, what about 'Sabka Saath Sabka Vikas'? This makes the question of satisfaction very relevant.

We find a highly diversified Muslim response in this regard. While a significant number of Muslims agree with the fact that the government has done a good job, there is an equally powerful segment of Muslim respondents who do not think that the development work has been satisfactory so far (Table 8.4). Although there is a crucial difference between Hindu and Muslim opinions on this issue, Muslim perceptions do not deviate significantly from the overall national opinion. This explains why only one-third of Muslims seem to be satisfied with the overall performance of the BJP government (Table 8.5).

Table 8.3: People's opinion on Modi-led central government performance with regard to controlling prices

	Opinion about the Modi government's performance in controlling price rise		
	Good	Bad	Average
Hindus	34	56	7
Muslims	28	60	9
Overall public opinion	33	57	7

All figures are in per cent. Figures may not add up to 100 due to rounding off. The rest did not respond.

(Source: CSDS–Lokniti Social and Political Barometer Survey 2023. N=7202)

Table 8.4: Opinion on Modi-led central government performance with regard to undertaking developmental work

	Opinion about the Modi government's performance in undertaking developmental work		
	Good	Bad	Average
Hindus	49	38	8
Muslims	41	45	9
Overall public opinion	47	40	8

All figures are in per cent. Figures may not add up to 100 due to rounding off. The rest did not respond.

(Source: CSDS–Lokniti Social and Political Barometer Survey 2023. N=7202)

Table 8.5: Satisfaction level with the BJP government

	Fully Satisfied	Somewhat Satisfied	Somewhat Dissatisfied	Fully Dissatisfied
Hindus	20	39	19	18
Muslims	5	31	24	33
Total	17	38	19	21

All figures are in percentages. Figures may not add up to 100 due to rounding off. The rest did not respond.

(Source: CSDS–Lokniti Social and Political Barometer Survey 2023. N=7202.)

Interestingly, we do not find any direct and clear correlation between economic dissatisfaction and political preferences. BJP seems to be the preferred political option at the national level as 39 per cent of respondents argue that they would vote for the party in the next Lok Sabha election (Table 8.6). This response is plausible because it validates the overall satisfaction level of different communities with regard to the BJP government's performance.

Although the Congress has emerged as the first choice for Muslims in this survey, the growing acceptability of the BJP among Muslims is quite noticeable. Almost 15 per cent of the Muslims claim that they would vote for BJP in 2024. According to CSDS–Lokniti National Election Study 2019, BJP received almost 9 per cent Muslim votes in the 17th Lok Sabha election. There is clearly an expected increase of six percentage points in Muslim support for the party. This is also true about the other parties, especially regional political formations. Almost 37 per cent of Muslims confirm that they would like to support the non-BJP, non-Congress formations in 2024. This diversity of Muslim political opinion certainly confirms that the idea of a Muslim vote bank does not exist at all.

Table 8.6: Expected voting

	Party you will vote for in Lok Sabha elections		
	Congress	**BJP**	**Others**
Hindus	26	45	26
Muslims	44	15	36
Total	29	39	28

All figures are in per cent. Figures may not add up to 100 due to rounding off. Others did not reveal their choices.

(Source: CSDS–Lokniti Social and Political Barometer Survey 2023. N=7202)

The figure of Narendra Modi has emerged as a decisive factor so far. While it is true that he is still the number one choice for the post of Prime Minster in the country, the popularity of Rahul Gandhi is also increasing gradually. The Muslim opinion on this question is again very diversified (Table 8.7). More than 40 per cent Muslims would like to see Rahul Gandhi as the PM of the country. However, a comparatively small, yet significant segment of Muslims favours Narendra Modi for the post of the PM.

Table 8.7: People's choice for PM face

	PM Choice		
	Narendra Modi	**Rahul Gandhi**	**Others**
Hindus	50	24	17
Muslims	16	40	31
Overall choice for PM	43	27	19

All figures are in per cent. Figures may not add up to 100 due to rounding off. The rest did not respond

(Source: CSDS–Lokniti Social and Political Barometer Survey 2023. N=7202)

It is worth noting here that almost 16 per cent of Muslims like Narendra Modi as a leader, while more than 38 per cent do not support this opinion. Interestingly, one-third of Muslim respondents do not want to answer this tricky question. It simply means that a section of Muslims would prefer to remain silent.

Table 8.8: Liking for Narendra Modi

	Like Modi	Don't Like	Neither like nor dislike
Hindus	45	21	23
Muslims	16	39	31
Total	40	23	25

All figures are in per cent. Figures may not add up to 100 due to rounding off. The rest did not respond.

(Source: CSDS–Lokniti *Social and Political Barometer Survey 2023.* N=7202)

This finding is also linked to Modi's skills as a leader (Table 8.8). A majority of Muslims recognize Modi's oratory skills as an important factor that makes him a popular leader. In fact, Muslim opinion beats the national average in this regard. It means that those Muslims who want to see Modi as the next PM are impressed with his communication skills (Table 8.9).

Three broad observations can be made on the basis of these findings. First, Muslim communities, like other social groups, are seriously concerned about a few crucial economic existential issues. The communal divide does not affect their perceptions about everyday life and resolve for collective survival. Second, Muslim communities still take the idea of political participation very seriously for their survival as a religious minority. They are highly uncomfortable with aggressive Hindutva, yet there is a constant search for the best possible political option. That is the

Table 8.9: Skills of Modi (only those who like Modi)

	Oratory skill	His idea of development	Hardworking/ Dedication	Charismatic/ Decisive	His policies	Others
Hindus	24	20	13	13	11	15
Muslims	29	17	11	13	14	12
Total	25	20	13	13	11	15

All figures are in per cent. Figures may not add up to 100 due to rounding off. The rest did not respond.

(Source: CSDS–Lokniti Social and Political Barometer Survey 2023. N=7202)

reason why a section of Muslims does not hesitate to support BJP. Finally, Muslims recognize the political importance of the figure of Narendra Modi. Again, there is a mixed response to this question. He is admired, disliked and even ignored. This diversity of opinion highlights the Muslim search for a peaceful and inclusive India.

IV

Participation as 'instrumental' action: Voters as Labharthis

Let us look at another kind of Muslim political attitude—participation as instrumental action. I take the UP Assembly Election in 2022 as an example for this discussion. The CSDS–Lokniti survey shows that Muslim voting demonstrates two very specific patterns in this election.[17] First, the rise of the BJP did not force Muslims to behave as a homogeneous political community. Muslims, unlike the popular perceptions, did not vote as a 'vote bank' in favour of a particular party. Although the SP–RLD coalition emerged as the first choice of Muslim voters, the other parties, including the BJP, did get Muslim votes. In fact, statistically speaking, the BJP has emerged as the second preferred party for Muslim voters in UP. Second, Muslim sociological diversity in terms of caste and class could not play any decisive role in this election. The Muslim upper castes along with Pasmanda and Dalit Muslim communities voted almost on similar lines (Table 8.10).

The class-wise Muslim voting trends also confirm this pattern. Muslims belonging to all economic classes voted for SP, though there was a minor variation in the voting behaviour of lower- and middle-class Muslims (Table 8.11). They seem to be slightly more open to the BJP.

Table 8.10: Social stratification and political choices in UP

	Congress	BJP+	BSP	SP+	Others
General Muslim	1	6	7	82	4
OBC Muslim	4	7	6	80	3
Total	3	7	6	79	5

Figures in per cent

(Source: CSDS–Lokniti UP Post-Poll survey 2022,
CSDS-Lokniti Data Unit)

Table 8.11: Class-divide and Muslim electoral responses

	BJP+	SP+	BSP	Congress	Others
Poor	7	77	7	3	6
Lower	8	83	4	2	3
Middle	8	77	6	5	4
Rich	2	79	10	1	8
Total	7	79	6	3	5

Figures in per cent

(Source: CSDS–Lokniti UP Post Poll survey 2022,
CSDS–Lokniti Data Unit)

These two rather conflicting findings encourage us to ask a few unconventional questions. Do Muslims vote only to defeat the BJP in a media-driven anti-Muslim environment? If yes, why do they vote despite knowing the fact that every political party is now keen to get Hindu votes? Do they get the benefits of the welfare policies offered by the state without any communal bias and prejudices? If yes, how do they react to it? If, not, what are their expectations from the state?

These second-order questions must be situated in the backdrop of two specific aspects of contemporary electoral politics: the 'charitable state model' and the electoral system called 'vote-management'. We have already discussed the idea of a charitable state in great detail in Chapter 2. The charitable state as a model of governance, as it has been argued, does not envisage welfarism as its fundamental political duty; instead, it offers benefits to citizens as acts of benevolence and generosity to bargain with them in the realm of competitive electoral politics. This is what most of the political observers noticed in UP. This phenomenon played an important role in the success of the BJP in UP (and other states). The party was able to reach out to voters directly in such a way that a clear political bargain could be materialized. The CSDS–Lokniti post-poll survey 2022 confirms that various schemes initiated by the UP government as well as the central government were able to influence the political choices of voters in UP.

Table 8.12: Welfare schemes and Muslims

Schemes	Total Households that have been benefited from . . .	Muslim Households that have been benefited from . . .	Muslim Households that have NOT been benefited from . . .
Free ration	80	80	20
Subsidized ration	60	51	48
Health insurance	30	22	77
Money in account	27	19	80

Assistance to build houses	21	16	84
Financial Assistance for marriages	15	13	87
Employment and Skill development	13	10	90

Figures in per cent

(Source: CSDS–Lokniti UP Post Poll survey 2022, CSDS–Lokniti Data Unit)

Table 8.12 shows that Muslims, like other communities, also received the benefits of various welfare schemes, especially in the post-Covid period. The distribution of free ration appears to be one of the most popular schemes of the government that reaching almost 80 per cent of Muslim households in the state. It simply means that the BJP government did not follow a discriminatory approach. However, we should not jump to the conclusion that the BJP's slogan 'Sabka Saath Sabka Vikas' functions as a policy paradigm.

Table 8.13: Caste/Community-wise voting

	Congress	BJP+	BSP	SP+	Others
Upper Caste	1	85	1	9	4
Jat	0	53	12	33	2
Yadav	1	12	1	83	3
Non-Yadav Voters	3	64	5	24	4

Dalit	2	28	50	14	6
Muslims	3	7	6	79	5
Others	7	55	8	22	8
Total	2	44	13	36	5

Figures in per cent

(Source: CSDS–Lokniti UP Post Poll Survey 2022,
CSDS–Lokniti Data Unit)

A close reading of the caste-community-wise voting pattern gives us a different picture (Table 8.13). The correlation between the labharthi phenomenon and the voting pattern of different caste-community groups is not entirely straightforward. The BJP received enthusiastic support from upper caste and non-Yadav OBCs. At the same time, it was able to attract voters from other social groups including Muslims. On the contrary, SP relied heavily on the Yadav–Muslim configuration.

It shows that the BJP was able to make the best use of the charitable state model. The economic benefits transferred directly to the voters by the government seem to authenticate the electoral promises made in BJP's *Sankalp Patra*. It does not, however, mean that every beneficiary social group overwhelmingly voted for the BJP. The voters also bargained with political parties and voted accordingly. In this sense, the Muslims of UP are not the only social group in the state that went against the BJP despite being a labharthi community.

This brings us to the second feature of the emerging electoral system, vote management. It is a fact that the BJP, at least officially, has not shown any interest in the Muslim vote to nurture its Hindutva constituency. The 80–20 remark made by Chief Minister Yogi Adityanath, in this sense, was right on target. Adityanath argued, 'The 80 per cent supporters will be on one side while 20 per cent will be on the other. I think 80 per cent will move forward with positive energy whereas 20 per cent have always opposed and will oppose further.'[18] Obviously, he did not use the terms 'Hindu' and 'Muslim'. Yet, he was able to communicate directly with his identified constituency of voters.

The BJP's Sankalp Patra also does not have any promise for minority communities. On the contrary, it justifies the party's apparent anti-Muslim narrative—love jihad laws, creation of anti-terrorist Commando Centre in a few Muslim-dominated districts and so on—in the name of *Sushasan* (good governance). This dominant Hindutva campaign, however, should not be exaggerated. BJP's electoral mechanism functions differently at the constituency level where the 80–20 binary does not work at all. The party relies on the idea of winnability; and precisely for that reason, it has to manage Muslim votes in such a way that its winning configurations are not unsettled. Muslim electoral responses must be understood in the backdrop of this vote-management technique championed by the BJP in recent years.

A clear religious polarization can be observed in those constituencies where Muslim population is more than 40 per cent (Table 8.14). However, we find a different trend in those districts where Muslims are less than 20 per cent. Muslims seem to be more flexible in these areas. This constituency-level Muslim voting also explains two possible facets of Muslim electoral politics. First, the Muslim voters adhere to the idea of winnability differently. They went for the best possible option available to them at the constituency level. That is the reason why a slightly higher number of Muslim candidates from established political parties won elections in 2022, especially from the Muslim-dominated areas.[19] Second, the Muslims did find an attraction in the speeches of Hyderabad MP Asaduddin Owaisi. However, his speeches could not compel them to vote for AIMIM candidates. This candidate-centric preference of Muslim voters explains the apparent failure of AIMIM. [20]

Table 8.14: Polarization at the constituency level

Voting in seats where Muslim population is....	BJP+		SP+		BSP		Congress		Others	
	Muslims	Hindus	Muslims	Hindus	Muslims	Hindus	Muslims	Hindus	Muslims	Hindus
Less than 20 per cent	14	51	74	30	4	13	5	2	3	4
20 per cent to 39 per cent	4	59	80	18	9	17	3	1	5	4
40 per cent or more	4	69	94	8	2	23	--	--	--	--

Figures in percentage

(Source: CSDS–Lokniti UP Post Poll survey 2022, CSDS–Lokniti Data Unit)

Muslim voting, nevertheless, cannot be reduced either to communal polarization or identity-specific considerations. Our survey shows that only 26 per cent of Muslims consider that the removal of the Adityanath government is an important electoral concern. For them, everyday life issues are more important than adhering to any imaginary anti-BJPism. This is why an ambiguous and overarching notion of 'development' appears to be the main reason behind their political enthusiasm (Table 8.15).

Table 8.15: The Muslim issues in UP

Issue	Overall response	Muslim Response
Development	38	29
Removal of government	12	26
Functioning of the government	10	4
Unemployment	7	8
Inflation	6	10
Other issues	24	20
No opinion	3	3

Figures in per cent

(Source: CSDS–2014 Lokniti UP Post Poll survey 2022, CSDS–Lokniti Data Unit)

Muslim voters have accepted the fact that Hindutva has emerged as the dominant narrative of Indian politics. They are fully aware that the non-BJP political parties cannot ignore the Hindutva-driven constituency of voters. It encourages them to consider the labharthi identity as a crucial factor in evaluating available political options at the constituency level.

In Lieu of a Conclusion

I

Connecting the dots

Let us recapitulate the main findings of this study to make sense of a brief and thematic 'history of the present' that I have tried to present in this book. I have pointed out in the Introduction that there is a need to go beyond the given explanatory templates because they are incapable of accommodating the multilayered Muslim identity. It is also asserted that a researcher must have a calm, dispassionate, sober, nuanced and open attitude towards political and social questions; at the same time, one must not give up his/her moral and political sensibilities to engage with public debates.

Chapter 1 makes three crucial suggestions to respond to these challenges. First, it is argued that a researcher must distance himself/herself from the people/communities he/she works on. Second, there is a need to pay close attention to the descriptive aspects of academic narratives. It is asserted that researchers interpret the communities/groups/phenomenon by employing various research strategies. These interpretative exercises are not based on what a researcher discovers in his/her research encounter; rather it is an outcome of his/her analytical investment in the subject of research. Thus, one must spell out the nature of these interpretative schemes for the sake of intellectual transparency. Finally, the nature of the arguments/ conclusions we draw from our research encounter is also very important. A researcher, therefore, is expected to produce intellectually informed and politically open arguments in such a manner that his/her readers may be able to draw their own political meanings. As a Muslim researcher, I do not want to give up my Islamic identity, and I do not want to speak only as a Muslim either.

The next chapter (Chapter 2) employs this analytical framework to examine the newness of the idea of New India. It shows that New India is an ideological–political doctrine, while 'Hindutva constitutionalism' is a mechanism to achieve it. This political configuration has produced a new kind of 'Charitable State', which envisages people as responsive citizens—citizens who do not expect the state to take the responsibility to provide jobs or long-term welfarism. Against this backdrop, I underline four postcolonial narratives of Indian politics—socialism, secularism, inclusion and Hindutva-driven nationalism. I argue that the doctrine of New India is an outcome of a 'rhetorical contestation', which is often celebrated in the public domain as the battle of 'ideologies'.

These two chapters provide a context to five thematic concerns—Muslim historical, Muslim cultural, Muslim liberal, Muslim social and Muslim political. We find a serious reconfiguration of these aspects of Indian Muslim identity in recent years. The political class (including a section of public intellectuals who claim to oppose Hindutva) seems to agree that the popular history of contemporary India cannot be written without problematizing the Muslim historical. This is also true about the controversial entity called the Muslim heritage.

The silence of non-BJP parties on the Gyanvapi issue shows that they subscribe to the Hindutva version of Muslim heritage and culture. I have tried to show the possibilities of thinking of the Muslim past and heritage in a different way. Chapter 3, for instance, has highlighted the fact that it is possible to liberate Muslim communities from the burden of ruler-centric elite Muslim history by employing the everyday resources of the living past. Similarly, it has been argued in Chapter 4 that Muslim communities do not recognize Aurangzeb as a religious symbol of Muslim cultures in India.

Chapter 5 problematizes the idea of Muslim religiosity and the impact of anti-Muslim discourse on it. This chapter has demonstrated that the amalgamation of global anti-Islamism and anti-Muslim communalism in the Indian context produced a new political phenomenon—Muslim politicophobia. This complicated representation of global Muslim identity, no doubt, has affected Muslim self-perceptions in a significant way. However, Muslim politicophobia has not yet become a determining factor of Islamic religiosity in India. I have argued that Muslim communities observe an imaginary dividing line between an inner domain of spirituality and the outer domain of politics. The inner domain is a site where new moral and ethical possibilities are explored within the framework of Islam. Aggressive Hindutva is placed in the outer domain to work out various survival strategies in a highly volatile anti-Muslim environment.

These survival strategies, interestingly, are different from the so-called Muslim issues. What are, then, the Muslim issues? How does a particular event/process/individual become a Muslim concern? How does a set of individuals emerge as Muslim stakeholders in public discourses? And finally, what is the mechanism that continues to produce Muslim issues over the years? Questions of this kind have been discussed rather systematically in Chapter 6 to critically assess the liberal Islam/cultural Muslim phenomenon. The chapter argues that it would be completely inappropriate to disregard the opinions and views of liberal Muslims. Their freedom of expression must always be respected. At the same time, the liberal Islam/cultural Muslim framework must accommodate subaltern voices—Pasmanda Muslims, Muslim women, and other marginalized sections of Muslim society—and the everyday forms of Islam. Otherwise, it would always remain elitist and exclusionary.

Social stratification among Muslims has emerged as an important political issue in contemporary India, especially after the rise of Pasmanda Muslim politics. Interestingly, the BJP has emerged as the most vocal campaigner for Pasmanda communities since 2021. I have tried to unpack this puzzling question in Chapter 7. The BJP's interest in Pasmanda Muslims stems from its highly professional political attitude. The party wants to expand its Hindutva constituency by projecting its pro-Pasmanda Muslim stand. That is the reason why the BJP does not talk about the complexities associated with legal-constitutional issues such as the controversial Presidential Order of 1950, which excludes Dalit Muslims and Dalit Christians from the Scheduled Caste list. I make a broad argument that Muslims invoke their Islamic Muslim identity not merely in religious terms. They also envisage themselves as a caste-like group in order to adjust to the wider caste-based environment. The social universe of Muslim communities, however, is governed by a different logic. They adhere to caste-based status hierarchies and even practice untouchability. The interplay between these two seemingly conflicting self-perceptions actually determines what I call the Muslim social.

This brings us to one of the central concerns of this book: Muslim political attitudes in New India. Chapter 8 shows that Muslims as citizens interact with other citizens and groups, they respond to public debates and assert their opinions, anxieties and criticisms. This form of participation has been described as 'participation as interaction'. The anti-CAA protests and

Muslim assessment of the Modi regime show that Muslims have not given up active peaceful politics. This chapter also underlines another form of Muslim engagement with politics, which I call participation as instrumental action. I argue that Muslims, like other social groups, take part in political processes, especially in elections, as stakeholders to secure certain material benefits. They behave like consumers/clients and respond to the welfare packages offered by the political parties. This explains the political significance of the labharthi phenomenon.

These findings offer us nuanced and multifaceted indications, which can further be evolved as explanatory claims to construct a big picture of our contemporary public life. More specifically, I make four tentative and open-ended arguments.

II

Argument 1: Muslim communities and the basics of Indian politics

I find the idea of the basic structure of Indian politics very useful. The doctrine of New India, the mechanism called Hindutva constitutionalism, the theme of India as the mother of democracy and the political time called Amrit Kaal are presented to us as a kind of departure from the established postcolonial political consensus. It is, in this sense, very crucial for us to think of those elements, which constitute the basic structure of Indian politics—a structure which cannot be changed by the political class. The official imagination of responsive citizens, which we have discussed in various chapters of this book rather extensively, is an important vantage point to develop this line of argument.

We know that the much-debated doctrine of the basic structure of the Constitution always revolves around the idea

of people. There is an agreement that the supremacy of the
Parliament is unquestionable because it represents the general
will of the people. In a speech delivered by Jagdeep Dhankhar,
the Vice President of India, this argument was reiterated
profoundly. He said, 'In [a] democratic society, "the basic" of
any "basic structure" has to be the supremacy of mandate of
people. Thus, the primacy and sovereignty of Parliament and
legislature is inviolable.'[1] The role of the judiciary as the most
authentic interpreter of the Constitution is also justified in the
name of the people.[2]

This overwhelming acceptability of the idea of people
actually relies on the two most powerful expressions of
peoplehood in the Indian context: voters and petitioners. The
regularity of free and fair elections and the active participation
of citizens as voters in electoral politics are evoked as people's
mandate. On the other hand, adherence to the established
legal-constitutional mechanisms to resolve conflicts is also seen
as people's faith in the judicial system.

The people, in this schema, emerge as an abstract collective
entity, which does not have any role to play in this so-called
standoff between the Parliament and the judiciary. This is the
reason why all serious discussions on the basic structure of the
Constitution remain indifferent towards the everyday meanings
of democracy, the perceptions of people about political
institutions, and their anxieties and expectations. The question
arises: can we think of a basic structure of Indian polity from
the point of view of the 'real people', the citizens?

Article 368 gives powers to Parliament to amend the
Constitution. The scope of such amendments, however, has
always been a contentious issue. According to one interpretation,
the amending powers of the Parliament are unrestricted and it
can revise, amend and even change any part of the Constitution.
There is also a counter argument. It is claimed that there are

certain key features of the Constitution, which determine its core identity. These features constitute what may be called the basic structure, which cannot be changed or altered by the Parliament. Hence, ideals such as the supremacy of the Constitution, the rule of law, separation of powers, judicial review, secularism, federalism, freedom and dignity of the individual and unity and integrity of the nation are often invoked to offer meaningfulness to this legal interpretation.[3]

This reasoning is useful to evaluate those elements of our postcolonial public life, which are cherished as fundamental political values. Precisely in this sense, three institutional features of the Indian political system (the supremacy of the Constitution, parliamentary form of government, and federalism) and two core principles (secularism and social justice) become more relevant from the point of view of our discussion in this book.

- The acceptability of the Constitution is a well-known fact of our public life. This acceptability, however, should not be reduced to the success of electoral outcomes. The Constitution has a remarkable public presence. It has been recognized as a symbol of protests and human liberation. Deprived and marginalized communities evoke the Constitution to assert their dignity and rights. The transformation of the Constitution from a 'rule book' to a 'manifesto of emancipation' certainly takes us beyond the highly rigid debate on the basic structure doctrine.

- This is also true about the parliamentary form of government. CSDS–Lokniti surveys show that a vast majority of Indians strongly believe that they would like to be governed by elected representatives. Although there is an inclination for a decisive and impactful leader, a parliamentary form of democracy based on competitive elections is recognized as the most suitable form of government for the country.

- Federalism is perhaps the most evident aspect of the basic outline of Indian politics. It is true that the Constitution gives more powers to the Union and the States are relatively weak. However, the people do not find this institutional division of power problematic. The last few elections have shown that Indian voters believe in strategic voting. They vote differently in different elections. The success of regional parties in powerful states over the years and the simultaneous rise of the BJP as the dominant party at the national level underline the actualities of our federal system.

- The public discussion on two core values—social justice and secularism—gives us an impression that these ideals have reached a saturation point and common people do not have any interest in them. This media-driven imagination is factually incorrect. It is true that Mandal-style politics of social justice has certainly declined. However, the assertion that the state must facilitate an egalitarian social order is still a powerful political impulse in the country. The presence of strong Dalit and Adivasi movements along with an impactful Indian feminist struggle influence the political discourse. No political party can ignore this comprehensive meaning of justice in its agenda, programme and policies.

- The post-2014 career of secularism as a political ideal, however, is slightly different. The success of the BJP has forced all political parties to give up the concept of secularism. It is believed that secular politics is counterproductive and it will help the BJP to consolidate its Hindutva constituency of voters. This assumption is absolutely incorrect. Various studies, including the Pew survey on religion in India, show that Indian communities still adhere to religious harmony and 'sarv dharm sambhav'—an expression of the Indian-specific form of secularism. This may be the reason why Indian Muslim communities still find secularism as an important metaphor for asserting their rights and dignity.

This brings us to our first argument. The reassessment of some of the core principles that constitute the operative outline of Indian politics is relevant to understanding the limits of contemporary debates. It shows that common people assert themselves silently by adhering to certain unwritten ideals and values. These ideals are formed and practised outside the institutional realm of the Parliament and judiciary. This is perhaps the most fundamental truth of our contemporary political life, which needs to be acknowledged seriously if we want to go beyond the given Hindu-Muslim divide.

II

Argument 2: The 'Crisis' of BJP

The electoral success of the BJP in post-2014 India cannot be disassociated from the multifaceted story of Indian democracy. We have tried to highlight the fact that the BJP, like any other party, follows the unwritten norms of electoral politics to persuade, attract and manage the voters to its advantage. This professional attitude has helped the party to establish Hindutva-driven nationalism as the dominant narrative of contemporary Indian politics.

This portrayal of the BJP's electoral triumph, however, is almost one-sided. The pro-BJP commentators celebrate the achievements of the Modi regime. They intentionally avoid any meaningful debate on the problems, challenges and possible crises the party might face in future. On the other hand, there is a serious and engaging discussion on democratic backsliding, which looks at the decline of institutional autonomy and growing authoritarian tendencies. This well-informed critique, interestingly, does not give adequate attention to the BJP's structural configuration and its political dynamics. As a result, there is no discussion on the BJP's institutional capability as a political party within the given framework of liberal democracy, especially when it is getting ready for the 2024 election under the leadership of Narendra Modi. Precisely for this reason, there is a need to engage with the BJP's internal problems for a better understanding of the present moment of democracy in India.

On the basis of our discussion in this book, four critical issues can be highlighted:

- The rise of Narendra Modi as 'the leader' of the BJP has certainly helped the party to manage its electoral victories over the years. In fact, the party has cultivated the image of Modi—not merely as a charismatic leader but also as a political symbol. In a way, the party has given Narendra Modi a twofold responsibility: he has to invent politically suitable images to maintain himself as the prime political symbol of the BJP. At the same time, he has to perform the task of an effective communicator to offer meanings to his own image. This over reliance on Narendra Modi seems to create an imbalance in the party organizations. On the one hand, there is an extraordinary burden on Narendra Modi to become the 'permanent performer' for the party; while on the other hand, there are no institutional efforts to nurture second-level leadership. This problem does not entirely stem from what is termed as 'centralization'. The party, it seems, is not invested in exploring the possibilities for an alternative backpack political package or strategy.

- The marginalization of intellectuals inside the party is the second critical issue. It is worth noting that the BJP always presents its ideology of cultural nationalism and integral humanism with great intellectual pride. Its leaders like Deendayal Upadhyaya, Atal Bihari Vajpayee, Balraj Madhok, L.K. Advani, and Arun Shourie were public intellectuals. The RSS has been instrumental in providing intellectual support to Jan Sangh as well as to the BJP. However, the intellectual class inside the party is not as vibrant as it used to be. Except for scholars like Rakesh Sinha or Ram Madhav, the BJP does not have serious intellectuals at the decision-making level. This evident demotion of the intelligentsia, it appears, will affect the institutionalized thinking culture of the party.

- The BJP's attitude towards the autonomy of established institutions is the third important issue. The debate on the appointment of judges, the use of independent investigating agencies against opposition leaders and even the disqualification of opposition MPs creates an impression that the BJP leadership wants to control the entire system in its favour. However, the problem is much more complicated. We should not forget that the BJP is an institution in itself. It is an inseparable constituent of two very powerful coalitions: the ideological coalition, the Sangh Parivar and the electoral coalition called the NDA. For the effective functioning of these coalitions, the BJP has to abide by institutional ethics of some kind. The growing tendency to disrespect or eventually

ignore the autonomy of institutions, in this sense, will
be counter-productive for the BJP in the long run.

- The induction of professional politicians from other
political parties is the fourth problem of the BJP. The
party has emerged as the most powerful political entity
in India since 2014. Professional politicians often
change political parties for the sake of individual upward
mobility. It was natural for some opposition leaders to
embrace the BJP for a better and secure political future.
Consequently, a large number of leaders from different
parties have joined the BJP. The overwhelming
enthusiasm of these professional politicians helped
the BJP to expand its mass base across the regions. It
was also beneficial for these leaders. They were able
to protect their own constituency of voters without
disrupting the BJP's aggressive electoral strategies.
However, this balance of power is not going to produce
desired results in the long run. The professional
politicians often prefer to associate themselves with the
dominant party. They have joined the BJP because they
want to take the maximum advantage of the Narendra
Modi phenomenon. These professional politicians will
not stay with the BJP if the party fails to retain power.
Karnataka and West Bengal are two very revealing
examples of this tendency.

The BJP, we must remember, does not merely represent a political
ideology; it is very much part of the democratic ecosystem of the
country. As the single dominant party, the challenges faced by
the BJP, are going to redefine the practicalities of our political
life. And for that reason, the crisis of the BJP would also have
an impact on Muslim political attitudes in future. This is the
second argument of the book.

III

Argument 3: Anti-Muslim violence and contemporary religiosity

The violence in 2023 in the Nuh and Mewat region of Haryana, which was followed by the demolition of houses and shops in and around the Gurugram area, has a wider political significance. It not merely underlines a set pattern of targeted violence but also points towards a much deeper crisis of our political life. The incident was officially recognized as communal violence— a form of collective action that is perpetrated across ethnic or communal lines.[4] By the same official logic, the use of bulldozers was legitimized for clearing alleged illegal encroachment. It is almost impossible to find any discriminatory angle in these overtly technical administrative moves.

Yet, most of the victims of this violence were Muslims; most of the houses/shops demolished by the authorities were owned by Muslims; most of the people who had to flee from this area after the violence were Muslims. And those who were socially and economically boycotted by a few village panchayats were also Muslims. It is a typical case where a particular community is systematically punished for being 'habitual troublemakers'. The Division Bench of Justices G.S. Sandhawalia and Harpreet Kaur Jeewan of Haryana and Punjab High Court also made a similar observation. They note: ' . . . the issue . . . arises whether the buildings belonging to a particular community are being brought down under the guise of law and order problem and an exercise of ethnic cleansing is being conducted by the State.'[5]

The standard liberal narrative, which we have discussed rather extensively in this book tells us that the state has become completely communal and Muslims are being targeted systematically to sustain and nurture aggressive Hindutva.

This explanation goes well with another powerful claim—
democratic and administrative backsliding. It is argued that
Indian democracy is declining under the BJP-dominated
NDA and anti-Muslim violence is an outcome of this political
deterioration. This line of reasoning is convincing. It might help
us in tracing the crucial links between emerging authoritarian
tendencies and the multifaceted violence against Muslims.

This explanation, however, has two limitations. First, it
overemphasizes the 2014 election and the rise of the Narendra
Modi-led BJP as a single, decisive, and determining factor
responsible for the communalization of state and administration
in the country. This is not true. The communal- and caste-
divide have always been an important aspect of our social life.
The political class—political parties and the groups associated
with them directly or indirectly—used these sociological fault-
lines to create legitimacy for itself in a variety of ways.

For a long period of time, communalism and casteism were
seen as challenges for the nation. The rise of Dalit and OBC
politics reconfigured this political consensus in the 1990s in
a significant way. Caste eventually became a recognized and
legitimate category for achieving social justice. This crucial
development went well with the basic philosophy of the Indian
constitution. At the same time, it did not pose any challenge
to the Congress-dominated narrative of secularism and social
inclusion.

Hindutva groups worked hard to appropriate the idea
of social justice. They evoked the historical and social
marginalization of Dalit and Hindu OBC communities to
create a new narrative of Hindu victimhood. The claim that
caste-based reservation is only meant for reforming Hinduism
is a good example of this political trajectory. The success of the
BJP post-2014, as we have argued in Chapter 3, has forced other
parties to accept this narrative as an ultimate reference point for

political negotiations. Instead of proposing any alternative idea of nationalism, they began to celebrate their 'Hindu pride'. That has been one of the reasons why non-BJP parties are hesitant to use the term 'secularism' to counter BJP's politics of Hindutva. The communalization of the state, in this sense, is inextricably linked to this new 'political consensus', which is more or less, accepted by the entire political class after 2014.

There is another problem with this explanation. The term 'democratic backsliding' is often used freely to describe a number of different and sometimes contradictory political trajectories. The decline of institutional autonomy, political centralization, and the authoritarian attitude of the ruling elite are seen as symbols of democratic backsliding in a strict comparative sense. It is assumed that there is an empirically observable benchmark for measuring the level of democratic performance of a regime. This assumption is factually problematic. Democracy in the Indian context cannot be restricted to free and fair elections. Instead, it is deeply associated with constitutional commitments to create a humane, rights-based egalitarian social order. Hence, measuring the multifaceted idea of Indian democracy based on an imagined checklist is analytically unhelpful. Communal violence against Muslims, for instance, is not a new phenomenon. There were serious riots in the past decades as well particularly when the Indian political system was not seen as a declining democracy. It simply means that the democratic backsliding framework does not offer any satisfactory explanation to make sense of the present form of anti-Muslim violence.

There is a need to go beyond this standard liberal explanation. The idea of religion is an important vantage point in this regard. Chapter 5 shows that the meanings of religion and religiosity have changed considerably in the last ten years. We have noted that contemporary religiosity is determined by a strange obsession with ritualism. A majority of Indians (that includes respondents belonging to all major religions) claim that it is very important to have public ceremonies for the birth of a child, public observance of death rituals and religious processions to mark important festivals to assert their faith.

This fascination for publicly displayed religiosity has two important implications. First, it reminds us that the crucial distinction between 'religion as a spiritual-moral force' and 'religion as an expression of identity' is gradually disappearing. Religions are primarily observed as 'competing ideologies'. Public assertion of religiosity is treated as an end in itself while there is no space for any discussion on moral religious values and for that matter, 'sarv dharm sambhav'.

Secondly, the public display of this competing religiosity corresponds directly to the dominant political consensus of our time—the Hindutva-driven nationalism. The demand to have *shoba yatras, maha panchayats* and celebrations of *kanvar yatras* by the state underlines the belief that religion can only be meaningfully observed if it is celebrated in public. The competitive dimension of this religiosity is equally crucial. The presence of green minarets of mosques and shrines, the public display of Namaz on roads, the recitation of Azan five times a day and a visibly Muslim figure in either in skull cap or in a Hijab contributes significantly to the given narrative of Hindu subjugation. This is precisely what has happened in the Nuh region. We must remember that Hindu communities are not mobilized for direct violence against Muslims. Instead, the public presence of Islam is used as a resource to create a fear psychosis among them. I argue that the failure of our political class is evident. They do not have the moral courage to question the emerging dogmatic nature of religion. They fear that such a moral intervention may disturb their electoral equation. This is perhaps one of the most serious challenges for our democratic sensibilities.

IV

Argument 4: Muslims and the enthusiasm of political society

The success of the Congress in the 2023 Karnataka assembly elections is seen as one of the outcomes of the Rahul Gandhi-led Bharat Jodo Yatra (BJY).[6] No one can deny the fact that the Yatra was one of the most serious political moves taken by the Congress establishment in the post-2014 period. It obviously helped the party to re-establish its presence at the grassroots level. However, the active role played by civil society organizations, people's movements and advocacy groups in this initiative has not been given adequate public attention.

A number of social activists, intellectuals and leaders of the grassroots movements not merely participated in the Yatra but also produced a moral justification for it. The moral claims generated during the BJY, in a way, influenced the Congress's campaign during this decisive election. However, the civil society groups always maintained a crucial distance from Congress to assert their autonomy. This principle-based moral support is a remarkable political phenomenon, which requires a systematic explanation.

It is worth noting that there has been media-driven propaganda against civil society groups—the NGOs working in the social sector are seen as foreign agents; the people's movements are rejected as anti-national factions; concerned citizens, academics and intellectuals are called 'Urban-Naxals'; and committed activists are addressed as *andolanjivi*. Then how do we explain the active participation of NGOs and grassroots organizations in support of a particular political party, in this case, the BJP's main target Congress?

The statement issued by a group of civil society organizations and individuals just before the BJY is very relevant to answer this question. This statement makes three arguments.

- First, the country is facing an unprecedented crisis when 'an overwhelming majority of the farmers and workers, Dalits and Adivasis, women and religious minorities faced such effective exclusion in the shaping of the nation's future'.
- Second, the BJY is seen as a mode to re-connect with people at that grassroots level simply to assert the constitutional values—liberty, equality, justice and fraternity.
- Finally, an important clarification is made with regard to the relative autonomy of people's movements. The statement says: '[I]n extending one-time support to an initiative like BJY, we do not tie ourselves to a political party or a leader, but simply affirm our readiness to set aside partisan considerations and stand with any meaningful and effective initiative to defend our constitutional republic'.[7]

This clarification, in a way, underlines the complex relationship between people's movements and political parties in postcolonial India. One may identify four watershed moments in this regard. The Jayaprakash Narayan-led anti-Emergency movement was the first important intervention that had far-reaching consequences. This movement did not merely pave the way for the creation of the Janata Party in 1977; it also strengthened civil liberties movements in the country. The People's Union for Democratic Rights (PUDR) and later the People's Union for Civil Liberties (PUCL), in this sense, were the outcome of the JP movement. Although the Janata Party experiment almost failed and Indira Gandhi's Congress (I) won the 1980 election comfortably, civil liberties organizations and people's movements continued to flourish as what political scientist Rajni Kothari calls 'non-party political formations'.[8] These grassroots-level movements also influenced mainstream electoral politics. Political parties had to acknowledge the issues raised by these struggles. The Chhattisgarh Mukti Morcha (CMM) a trade union movement led by an iconic figure, Shankar Guha Niyogi, is a good example to elaborate on this point. Despite being a trade union movement, CMM did not ignore the significance of electoral politics. Morcha leaders contested elections and won two assembly seats in the mid-1980s. Around the same time, the Narmada Bachao Andolan (NBA) against the Sardar Sarovar Dam emerged as an important reference point for a democratic and just notion of sustainable development. The movement gave a new meaning to environmental justice. The NBA relied heavily on the democratic values enshrined in the Constitution to justify its campaign for the rehabilitation of displaced communities.

The formation of the National Alliance for People's Movements (NAPM) was the second important trajectory. The NAPM was formed in the early 1990s by a variety of people's movements to offer democratic resolve to the challenges posed by economic globalization and aggressive communal politics. This development also contributed to the ever-expanding NGO sector, which later came to be known as the Third Sector (the government and the private sector being the other two). Hence, the civil liberties and democratic rights organizations, the grassroots people's movements, Dalit, Adivasi and women's movements and NGOs actually formed the contours of the sphere, which may be called an extended version of the 'political society'—a crucial concept used by political theorist Partha Chatterjee to describe the politics of the 'governed'.[9]

The constituents of this highly diversified political society were involved in a deep politics of democratic rights. It does not, however, mean that they were apolitical; instead, they maintained a crucial distance from party politics in the 1990s. That might be the reason why we do not find any collective effort by the people's movements to intervene in the arena of electoral politics more directly.

The anti-corruption movement led by Anna Hazare in the early 2010s was the third watershed moment. Although this campaign was primarily concerned with the issue of institutional corruption, it received overwhelming support from people's movements of all kinds. The formation of the Aam Aadmi Party (AAP) was the natural outcome. AAP tried to accommodate the aspirations of people's movements in its constitution to promote a new principle-based politics. However, the AAP could not maintain this moral-intellectual relationship with people's movements and eventually became a typical professional party. In fact, the party constitution was also amended for purely practical purposes.[10]

The present moment of politics, in a sense, is a result of this disenchantment. The constituents of the political society have realized that they have to take a principled position in the arena of mainstream politics. The support given to BJY is a manifestation of this resolve. This is exactly what Partha Chatterjee hopes in the concluding part of his remarkable book, *I am the People*. He writes:

> There must . . . be a more long-term project of producing, circulating, and instilling in the popular consciousness a narrative of social transformation. In particular, the challenge posed by right-wing populism . . . cannot be met by electoral tactics alone. . . . Who will begin this counter-hegemonic project? Critique, imagination, and pedagogy are part of the intellectual's calling. As Gramsci's notebooks continue

to remind us, intellectuals who are able to turn their ideas into the stuff of popular education lay the groundwork for hegemonic transformation.[11]

The extended sphere of political society, it appears, answers the question posed by Chatterjee here. The Muslim political attitude, which we discussed in great detail in Chapter 8, corresponds to this big picture of our vibrant political society. I argue that the debate on the future of democratic politics in India should not be reduced merely to juicy discussions on TINA (there is no alternative) factor or the desirability of opposition unity in 2024. Instead, the deep politics of civil society groups and people's movements must be taken seriously to capture the future trajectories of Indian democracy.

V

Argument 5: The 'way out': Garam Hava

One of the most constructive critiques of New India has come from Yogendra Yadav. His notion of India's *Swadharma* underlines the intrinsic unity between the distinctiveness of Indian democracy and its cultural acceptance. Yadav's conceptualization of Swadharma is not merely about the glorious Indian civilization, which Nehru aims to rediscover in his *Discovery of India*; nor does he reduce it to the constitutional ideals, which are often cherished in the name of political correctness. Instead, he defines India's Swadharma as *Bharat ka Iman*—an element which captures the uniqueness of our democratic experiences in the post-1950 period.[12]

There are three facets of Swadharma, which tend to redefine the much-celebrated Western political ideals—democracy, diversity and development—in the Indian context.

- According to Yadav, India convinced the world that democracy could be practised in conditions of deep disadvantage and lack of formal education. In this sense, Indians democratized the idea of democracy by transforming it into a public virtue.
- This is also true about diversity. Yadav suggests that the Indian idea of diversity has not been about celebrating cultural/religious differences. Instead, diversity in the Indian context means 'acceptance of radically different ways of being'. Hindus and Muslims can live together peacefully as citizens without compromising their religious beliefs.
- The idea of development is also redefined in the same way. Yadav argues that development is not about GDP growth rate or per capita income. For him, 'what is distinctive about our contribution to thinking about development is the idea of the last person first'.[13]

This conceptualization of Swadharma is invoked in two different ways. First, it is established as a political–moral principle by Yadav to reject the political foundation of Modi's New India. It is argued that the CAA and the removal of Article 370 go against the Indian conceptions of diversity. Similarly, the allegedly lethargic and irresponsive attitude of the government in the economic sphere is shown as a political betrayal. However, there is a constructive proposal in it. Yadav makes a persuasive plea to evolve a *Bharat Jodo Andolan* to channel the political energies generated by the people's struggles to achieve a peaceful and democratic social transformation.[14] The active participation of people's movements in the Bharat Jodo Yatra, in a way, underlines the actual manifestation of this creative intellectual proposal. It is clear that *New India* aims to produce obedient, disciplined and governable citizens.

It relies on a power-centric interpretation of the Constitution and a Hindutva-driven nationalism. The idea of Swadharma not merely rejects New India on moral-political grounds but also proposes a humane, inclusive and participatory vision to achieve what could be called a 'believable idea of Just India'.

In my view, this conceptualization is very useful to get rid of the 'liberal versus Hindutva' binary. Swadharma does not adhere to a one-dimensional Muslim identity. Muslims like me still find solace in creative resolve because it gives us hope and does not ask us to speak as a Muslim.

It reminds me of M.S. Saathyu's film *Garam Hawa* (1973). In the final scene of the film, set in the days following independence, young and unemployed Sikandar Mirza (Farooq Shaikh), whose family has finally decided to move to Pakistan after facing communal prejudices of all kinds, refuses to go.[15]

Sikander eventually joins a group of demonstrators demanding equality and radical pro-people transformation. I think Sikander is right—the fight against anti-Muslimism cannot be separated from the wider struggle for social justice and economic equality. So, the answer lies in a radically revised template of progressive politics—one which allows the individuals like me to critique economic injustice and social inequalities while adhering to my conception of a liberative Islam.

References and Bibliography

Aggarwal, Partap C.1966. 'A Muslim sub-caste of north India: Problems of cultural integration'. *Economic and Political Weekly*: 159–161

Ahmad, Imtiaz. 1972. 'For a sociology of India'. *Contributions to Indian Sociology* 6. no. 1: 172–178

Ahmad, Imtiaz. 2005. 'India and the Muslim World'. *Economic and Political Weekly*: 819–822

Ahmad, Imtiaz. ed. 1978. *Caste and Social Stratification Among Muslims in India*. Manohar

Ahmad, Imtiaz. ed. 1981. *Ritual and Religion among Muslims in India*. Delhi: Manohar

Ahmad, Imtiaz. 2006. 'Why is the Veil such a Contentious Issue?'. *Economic and Political Weekly*: 5037–5038

Ahmad, Irfan. 2003. 'A different jihad: Dalit Muslims' challenge to Ashraf hegemony'. *Economic and Political Weekly*: 4886–4891

Ahmad, Irfan. 2009. *Islamism and Democracy in India: The Transformation of Jamaat-e-Islami*: Princeton University Press

Ahmad, S. Shamim, and A.K. Chakravarti. 1981. 'Some regional characteristics of Muslim caste systems in India'. *GeoJournal* 5: 55–60

Ahmed, Hilal, Vijaisri, Priyadarshini, Dubey, Abhay Kumar. 2012. The Centre and Indian Realities: Interview with Rajni Kothari. *Seminar*, 639, November 2012

Ahmed, Hilal. 2012. 'Fictions of Intellectual Politics: Manto', *Social Scientist*, Vol. 472–473. Pp. 31–41

Ahmed, Hilal. 2013. 'Asghar Ali Engineer: Emancipatory Intellectual Politics'. *Economic and Political Weekly*, Vol. XLVII NO. 22. Pp. 20–22

Ahmed, Hilal. 2016. 'Exploring Muslim Modernities: Public Presence of Mosques in Delhi and London', Anwar Alam, Konrad Pedziwiatr (Eds), *Muslim Minorities in Europe and India: Politics of Accommodation of Islamic Identities*. New Century publications, Delhi. Pp. 111–132

Ahmed, Hilal. 2019. *Siyasi Muslims: A Story of Political Islams in India*. New Delhi: Penguin Random House India

Ahmed, Hilal. 2020. 'Discourse(s) of Dawa in postcolonial India'. Weismann. Itzchak and Malik, Jamal (eds.) *Culture of Dawa: Islamic Preaching in the Modern World*. University of Utah Press: Salt Lake City. Pp. 31–46

Ahmed, Hilal. 2020a. Making Sense of India's Citizenship Amendment Act 2019: Process, Politics, Protest. *Asie Visions*. No. 114. ifri. https://www.ifri.org/en/publications/notes-de-lifri/asie-visions/making-sense-indias-citizenship-amendment-act-2019-process

Ahmed, Hilal. 2022. 'Muslim Presence in *Padamavat*' in Ira Bhaskar and Richard Allen (eds). *Bombay Cinema's Islamicate Histories*. Hyderabad: Orient Blackswan. Pp. 182–200

Ahmed, Hilal. 2022. 'New India, Hindutva Constitutionalism, and Muslim Political Attitudes'. *Studies in Indian Politics* 10, no. 1: 62–78

Ahmad, Imtiaz. 1967. 'Indian Muslims and electoral politics'. *Economic and Political Weekly*: 521–5

Ahmed, Shahab. 2016. *What is Islam: The Importance of Being Islamic*. Princeton and Oxford, Princeton University Press

Ahmed, Hilal. 2014. *Muslim Political Discourse in India: Monuments, Memory, Contestation*. London, New Delhi: Routledge

Ahmed, Hilal. 2019c. Communal Violence, Electoral Mobilization, and Muslim Representation: Muzaffarnagar 2013–14; Irfan Ahmad and Pralay
Kanungo (eds.). *The Algebra of Warfare-Welfare: Along View of India's 2014 Election*. Delhi: Oxford University Press. Pp. 163–196

Alam, Arshad. 2007. 'New Directions in Indian Muslim Politics the Agenda of All India Pasmanda Muslim Mahaz'. *Contemporary Perspectives*. Vol 1. No.2. 130–143

Alam, Arshad. 2009. 'Challenging the Ashrafs: The Politics of Pasmanda Muslim Mahaz'. *Journal of Muslim Minority Affairs*. Vol 29. No.2. Pp. 171–181

Alam, Arshad. 2013. 'Islam and Religious Pluralism in India'. *India International Centre Quarterly*, *40*(3/4). Pp. 47–64. http://www.jstor.org/stable/24394389

Alam, Javeed. 2008. 'The Contemporary Muslim Situation in India: A Long-Term View'. *Economic and Political Weekly*, 43(2). Pp. 45–53. http://www.jstor.org/stable/40276902

Alam, Mohd Sanjeer. 2009. 'Whither Muslim Politics?'. *Economic and Political Weekly*. Pp. 92–95

Ali, Manjur. 2022. 'Politics of "Pasmanda" Muslims: a case study of Bihar'. *History and Sociology of South Asia* 4. No. 2. Pp. 129–144

Ali, Syed. 2022. 'Collective and elective ethnicity: Caste among urban Muslims in India'. *In Sociological Forum*. Vol. 17. Pp. 593–620. Kluwer Academic Publishers–Plenum Publishers.

Ambedkar, B.R. 1943. *Pakistan or the Partition of India*. http://www.columbia.edu/itc/mealac/pritchett/00ambedkar/ambedkar_partition/. Accessed on 9 August 2023

Ambedkar, B.R. *Annihilation of Caste*. https://ccnmtl.columbia.edu/projects/mmt/ambedkar/web/readings/aoc_print_2004.pdf. Accessed on 5 June 2020

Anderson, Edward. 2015. 'Neo-Hindutva': the Asia House M.F. Husain campaign and the mainstreaming of Hindu nationalist rhetoric in Britain. *Contemporary South Asia*. Vol. 23. No. 1. Pp. 45–66

Ansari, Ali Anwar. 2023. *Masawat ki Jung (The Battle for Equality)*. New Delhi: Forward Press

Ansari, Ghaus. 1960. *Muslim Caste in Uttar Pradesh: A study of Cultural Contact*. Lucknow: Ethnographic and Folk Culture Society UP

Ansari, Khalid Anis. 2009. 'Rethinking the Pasmanda movement'. *Economic and Political Weekly*. Pp. 8–10

Ansari, Khalid Anis. 2021. 'Pluralism and the Post-Minority Condition: Reflections on the "Pasmanda Muslim" Discourse in North India'. Santos, Boaventura de Sousa, Martins, Bruno Sena (eds.). *The Pluriverse of Human Rights: The Diversity of Struggles for Dignity*. New York and London: Routledge. Pp. 106–127

Ansari, Khalid Anis. 2023. 'Revisiting the Minority Imagination: An Inquiry into the Anticaste Pasmanda-Muslim Discourse in India'. *Critical Philosophy of Race* 11. No.1. 120–147

Arosoaie, Aida. 2018. 'Understanding the creation and radicalisation of the Students Islamic Movement of India (SIMI) and the Indian Mujahideen (IM)'. *South Asia: Journal of South Asian Studies* 41, no. 3. Pp. 519–534.

Arshad, Madani and Sulaiman, Mohammad. 1992. *Preface to the Quaran Sharif: Anuwad and Vyakhya* (Hindi. Translation and Explanation). Delhi: Jamiat Ulama-e-Hindi

Asad, Talal. 2001. 'Reading a Modern Classic: W.C. Smith's "The Meaning and End of Religion" *History of Religions*'. Vol. 40. No. 3 (Feb.). Pp. 205–222

Bajpai, Rochana, and Adnan Farooqui. 2018. 'Non-extremist outbidding: Muslim leadership in majoritarian India'. *Nationalism and Ethnic Politics*. 24. No. 3. Pp. 276–298

Bajpai, Shailaja. 2021. 'Taliban, Taliban, Taliban. Indian news channels serve 'exclusive' interviews, source-less videos'. *Print*. https://theprint.in/opinion/telescope/taliban-taliban-

taliban-indian-news-channels-serve-exclusive-interviews-source-less-videos/726424/ accessed on 30 March 2022.

Banerjee, Mukulika. 2014. *Why India Votes? Exploring the Political in South Asia.* Routledge.

Baumann, Gerd. 1996. *Contesting Culture: Discourses of Identity in Multi-Ethnic London.* Cambridge: Cambridge University Press.

Bellamy, Carla. 2021. 'Being Muslim the Chhipa way: Caste identity as Islamic identity in a low-caste Indian Muslim community'. *Contributions to Indian Sociology.* 55. No. 2. Pp. 224–253.

Bhargava, Rajeev (ed). 2009. *Politics and Ethics of the Indian Constitution.* Oxford University Press

Bhargava, Rajeev. 2017. 'Constitutional or party-political secularism?' *The Hindu.* https://www.thehindu.com/opinion/op-ed/constitutional-or-party-political-secularism/article19436067.ece. Accessed on 15 Fenruary 2024.

Bhattacharya, Neeladri. 2008. 'Predicaments of Secular Histories'. *Public Culture.* 20(1). Pp. 57–73

Bilgrami, Akeel. 2018. 'Identity'. J.M. Bernstein, Adi Ophir, Ann Laura Stoler (eds.). *Political Concepts: A Critical Lexicon.* Fordham University Press. Pp. 159–166

Bleich, Erik. 2012. 'Defining and Researching Islamophobia'. *Review of Middle East Studies.* Vol. 46, No. 2 (Winter). Pp. 180–189

Chatterjee, Partha. 2019. *I am the People: Reflections on Popular Sovereignty Today.* Columbia University Press

Chatterjee, Partha. 2008. 'Democracy and Economic Transformation in India'. *Economic and Political Weekly.* 43(16). Pp. 53–62.

Clifford, James. George E Marcus. 1986. *Writing Culture: The Poetics and Politics of Ethnography.* Berkeley CA: University of California Press.

Cow Protection Legislation and Vigilante Violence in India. 2021. *Armed Conflict Location & Event Data Project.*

Das, Samir Kumar (ed). 2015. 'Introduction'. *In India: Democracy and violence.* Pp. 1–28. Oxford University Press.

Della Porta, Donatella, and Heinz–Gerhard Haupt. 2022. 'Patterns of radicalization in political activism: An introduction'. *Social Science History.* 36. No. 3. Pp 311–320

Desai, Madhuri. 2003. 'Mosques, Temples, and Orientalists: Hegemonic Imaginations in Banaras'. *Traditional Dwellings and Settlements Review.* 15. No. 1. Pp. 23–37. http://www.jstor.org/stable/41758028

Desai, Madhuri. 2019. 'The Vishweshwur temple and Gyan Vapi mosque: entangled histories in Banaras'. *Contested Holy Cities.* Pp. 63–80. Routledge

Deshpande, Satish. 2009. *Dalits in the Muslim and Christian Communities A Status Report on Current Social Scientific Knowledge.* New Delhi: National Commission for Minorities, Government of India

DeSouza, Peter Ronald. 2015. 'Living Between Thought and Action'; Thapar, Romina (ed). 2015. *The Public Intellectual in India.* New Delhi: Aleph. Pp. 79–100

Desouza, Peter. R, Ahmed, Hilal, Alam, Mohamad Sanjeer. 2019. *Democratic Accommodations: Minorities in contemporary India.* Bloomsbury: New Delhi and London

Eaton, Richard M. 2000. *Essays on Islam and Indian History.* Delhi: Oxford University Press

El Kurd, Dana, 2018. 'Religiosity and its Political Effects'. *AlMuntaqa.* Vol. 1. No. 2 (August). Pp. 81–89

Emmerich, Arndt. 2019. 'Political Education and Legal Pragmatism of Muslim Organizations in India'. *Asian Survey.* 59. No. 3. Pp. 451–473

Emmerich, Arndt. 2020. *Islamic Movements in India: Moderation and its discontents.* London and New York: Routledge

Farooqui, Adnan. 2020. 'Political representation of a minority: Muslim representation in Contemporary India'. *India Review*. 19(2). Pp. 153–175. //doi.org/10.1080/14736489. 2020.1744996

Fazalbhoy, Nasreen. 2005. 'Sociology and Muslims in India: Directions, Trends, Prospects'. *Sociological Bulletin*. 54(3). September–December. Pp. 496–513

Foucault, Michel. 1991. *Discipline and Punish* (Penguin Social Sciences) (A. Sheridan, [trans.]). New York: Penguin Books.

Foucault, Michel. 2020. *Wrong-Doing, Truth-Telling: The Function of Avowal in Justice* (F. Brion & B.E. Harcourt [eds.]; S.W. Sawyer, [trans.]). University of Chicago Press

Gandhi, M.K. 1938. *Hind Swaraj*. Ahmadabad: Navjivan Trust

Gautier, Laurence, and Julien Levesque. 'Introduction: historicizing Sayyid-ness: social status and Muslim identity in South Asia'. *Journal of the Royal Asiatic Society*. 30. No. 3 (2020). Pp. 383–393

Gopal Sarvepalli (ed.). 1990. *Anatomy of Confrontation: The Babri-Masjid-Ramjanmabhumi Issue*. Delhi: Penguin Random House India.

Goradia, Prafull. 2002. *Hindu Masjid*. Delhi: Targett.

Gupta, Akhil. 1995. 'Blurred boundaries: the discourse of corruption, the culture of politics, and the imagined state'. *American ethnologist*. 22. No. 2. Pp. 375–402.

Habib, Irfan. 2012. *Jihad or Ijtihad: Religious Orthodoxy And Modern Science In Contemporary Islam*. New Delhi: HarperCollins Publishers India

Hasan, Mushirul. 1997. *Legacy of a Divided Nation: India's Muslims since Independence*. London: Hurst &Co

Hasan, Mushirul. 2002. 'Textbooks and Imagined History: The BJP's Intellectual Agenda'. *India International Centre Quarterly*. Vol. 29. No. 1 (SUMMER). Pp. 75–90

Heath, Oliver, Gilles Verniers, and Sanjay Kumar. 'Do Muslim voters prefer Muslim candidates? Co-religiosity and voting behaviour in India'. *Electoral Studies.* 38 (2015). Pp. 10–18

Iqbal, Muhammad. 2006. *Shikwa* (English Translation). http://oldpoetry.com/opoem/30200

Iyer, Sriya. 2018. *Economics of Religion in India.* Cambridge, Massachusetts: The Belknap Press of Harvard University Press.

Jaffrelot Christophe (eds.). 2019. *Majoritarian state: How Hindu nationalism is changing India.* Pp. 101–116. London: Harper Collins.

Jayal, Niraja Gopal. 1994. 'The Gentle Leviathan: Welfare and the Indian State'. *Social Scientist.* Vol. 22. No. 9/12 (September–December). Pp. 18–26.

Jeffery, Robin and Sen, Ronojoy (eds). 2014. *Being Muslim in South Asia: Diversity and Daily Life.* New Delhi: Oxford University Press

Kalyani Devaki Menon. 2022. 'Life, labour, and dreams: one woman's life in Old Delhi'. *Contemporary South Asia.* Vol. 30. No:1. Pp. 87–100

Kaviraj, Sudipta. 2010. *Imaginary Institution of India: Politics and Ideas.* New York: Columbia University Press

Kaviraj, Sudipta. 2013. 'Languages of Secularity'. *Economic and Political Weekly.* 48. No. 50. Pp. 93–102

Khalidi, Omar. 1993. 'Muslims in Indian Political Process: Group Goals and Alternative Strategies'. *Economic and Political Weekly.* 28(1/2). Pp. 43–54. http://www.jstor.org/stable/4399279

Khosla, Madhav. 2020. *India's founding moment: The constitution of a most surprising democracy.* Harvard University Press

Kim, Heewon. 2019. *The Struggle for Equality: India's Muslims and Rethinking the UPA Experience.* Cambridge: Cambridge University Press

Kothari, Rajni. 1984. 'The Non-Party Political Process'. *Economic and Political Weekly. 19*(5). Pp. 216–224

Kritzman, Lawrence. 1988. 'Power and sex: An interview with Michel Foucault' in Kritzman, L.D. (ed.). *Michel Foucault: Politics, Philosophy, Culture: Interviews and Other Writings*, 1977–1984. New York: Routledge.

Kumar Anand. 2013. 'A Constructive Challenge to the Political Class: The Aam Aadmi's Party'. *Economic and Political Weekly.* Vol. 48. No. 7 (16 February 2013). Pp. 11–15

Lazzaretti, Vera. 2023. 'Ayodhya 2.0 in Banaras? Judicial discourses and rituals of place in the making of Hindu majoritarianism'. *Contemporary South Asia.* Pp. 1–18

Levesque, Julien. 2020. 'Muslim politics and the 2020 Bihar election'. *India Forum.* Retrieved 12 December 2020 from https://www.theindiaforum.in/article/muslim-politics-and-2020-bihar-election

Levitsky, Steven. Ziblatt, Daniel. 2018. *How Democracies Die?* London: Penguin Random House UK

Lijphart, Arend. 1996. 'The puzzle of Indian democracy: A consociational interpretation'. *American Political Science Review.* 90. No. 2. Pp. 258–268

Madan, Triloki Nath. 2011. 'Islam: The universal and the particular'. *Sociological Traditions: Methods and Perspectives in the Sociology of India.* SAGE Publication

Madani, Arshad. Sulaiman, Mohammad. 1992. *Preface to the Quaran Sharif: Anuwad and Vyakhya* (Hindi. *Holy Quran: Translation and Explanation*). Delhi: Jamiat Ulama-e-Hindi

Menon, Aditya. 2019. 'Dear Muslims in Modi's India: Embrace politics, don't shun it'. *Quint.* https://www.thequint.com/voices/opinion/indian-muslims-way-ahead-narendra-modi-asaduddin-owaisi-jharkhand-lynching, accessed 15 February 2024

Metcalf, Barbara D. 2006. 'Imrana: Rape, Islam, and law in India'. *Islamic studies*. 45. No. 3. Pp. 389–412

Metcalf, Barbara D. 2009. *Islam in South Asia in Practice* (B. D. Metcalf, Ed.). Princeton University Press

Mines, Mattison. 1972. 'Muslim Social Stratification in India: The Basis for Variation'. *Southwestern Journal of Anthropology*. 28. No. 4. 333–49. http://www.jstor.org/stable/3629316

Müller, Jan Werner. 2016. *What is Populism*. Philadelphia: University of Pennsylvania Press

Nair, Sobhana, K. 2020. 'Congress, RJD too scared to talk about CAA, NRC: Asaduddin Owaisi'. *The Hindu*. Retrieved 12 December 2020, from https://www.thehindu.com/elections/bihar-assembly/congress-rjd-too-scared-to-talk-about-caa-nrc-owaisi/article33077148.ece

Nandy, Ashis. Trivedi, Shikha. Mayaram, Shail. Yagnic, Achyut. 1995. *Creating a Nationality: The Ram Janambhuni Movement and the Fear of the Self*. Delhi: Oxford University Press

Narayan, Jayaprakash. 1959. *A Plea for the Reconstruction of the Indian polity*. Akhil Bharat Sarva Seva Sangh Prakashan

Nigam, Aditya. 2008. 'The implosion of "the political"'. *Journal of Contemporary Thought*, 27. https://criticalencounters.net/2009/05/14/the-implosion-of-%E2%80%98the-political%E2%80%99/

Palshikar, Suhas. 2019. 'Toward hegemony: The BJP beyond electoral dominance' in A.P. Chaterji, T.B. Hansen, & C. Jaffrelot (eds.). *Majoritarian State: How Hindu Nationalism Is Changing India*. Pp. 101–116. New Delhi: Harper Collins

Pandey, Anurag. 2007. 'Communalism and separatism in India: an analysis'. *Journal of Asian and African Studies*. 42. No.6. Pp. 533–549

Parveen, Nazima. 2021. *Contested Homelands: Politics of Space and Identity*, London: Bloomsbury Academic

Pavan K. Varma. 2021. *The Great Hindu Civilization: Achievement, Neglect, Bias and the Way Forward*, Chennai: Westland Non-fiction

Prakash, Gyan. 1990. Writing Post–Orientalist Histories of the Third World: Perspectives from Indian Historiography. *Comparative Study in Society and History* (April)

Prasad, Shubha Kamala and Nooruddin, Irfan. 2019. 'I am New India' in Maiko Ichihara, Eunjung Lim, Shubha Kamala Prasad, Irfan Nooruddin, R.M. Marty M. Natalegawa and Daniel Twining, *Asianism and Universalism: The Evolution of Norms and Power in Modern Asia.* Center for Strategic and International Studies (CSIS). Pp. 21–29

Ramachandran, Sudha. 2020. Hindutva Violence in India: Trends and Implications. *Counter Terrorist Trends and Analyses.* Vol. 12. No. 4. Pp. 15–20

Rao, Nandini. 2020. 'Interpreting silences: symbol and history in the case of Ram Janmabhoomi/Babri Masjid' in *Social construction of the past.* Pp. 154–164). Routledge

Rao, Rahul. 2020. 'Nationalisms by, against and beyond the Indian state'. *Radical Philosophy.* 2.07. Pp. 17–27. https://www.radicalphilosophy.com/commentary/nationalisms-by-against-and-beyond-the-indian-state

Rao, Rahul. 2020. 'Nationalisms by, against and beyond the Indian state'. *Radical Philosophy*, 2.07, 17–27. https://www.radicalphilosophy.com/commentary/nationalisms-by-against-and-beyond-the-indian-state

Robinson, Francis. 1977. 'Nation formation: the Brass thesis and Muslim separatism'. *Journal of Commonwealth & Comparative Politics.* 15. No.3. Pp. 215–230

Saha, Anjan. 2023. 'Almighty as Litigant: Ram Janmabhoomi Case and the Concept of juristic personhood of temple deities in India'. *International Journal of English Literature and Social Sciences (IJELS)* 8. No. 2

Sajjad, Mohammad. 2014. *Muslim politics in Bihar*. London: Routledge.

Salam, Zia Us. 2020. *Inside the Tablighi Jamaat*. New Delhi: Harper Collins

Salam, Ziya Us. 2020. *Shaheen Bagh: From a Protest to a Movement*. New Delhi: Bloomsbury

Santhosh, R., and Dayal Paleri. 2021. 'Crisis of secularism and changing contours of minority politics in India: Lessons from the analysis of a Muslim political organization'. *Asian Survey*. 61. No. 6. Pp. 999–1027

Savarkar, V.D. 1969. *Hindutva: Who is a Hindu?* Bombay: Veer Savarkar Prakashan

Sayyed Zainuddin. 2003. 'Islam, Social Stratification and Empowerment of Muslim OBCs'. *Economic and Political Weekly*. 38(46). Pp. 4898–4901. http://www.jstor.org/stable/4414285

Scaff, Lawrence A. 1975. 'Two concepts of political participation'. *Western Political Quarterly*. 28. No. 3. Pp. 447–462

Shabir, Aamina, and Tanveer Ahmad Khan. 2022. 'Media as an Instrument of Reflection or Distortion of the Real Life Problems of Muslim Women in India'. *Journal of Social Inclusion Studies*. 8. No. 1: 86–96

Shakir, Moin. 1979. 'Religion and Politics: Role of Islam in Modern India'. *Economic and Political Weekly*. Pp. 469–474. http://www.jstor.org/stable/4367365

Sökefeld, Martin. 2001. Reconsidering Identity. *Anthropos*. Bd. 96. H. 2. Pp. 527–544

Sreedhar Rao, K. 2008. 'India and the Threat of Radical Islam'. *Strategic Analysis*. 32(5). 721–728

SWJN (Selected Works of Jawaharlal Nehru) 1972. New Delhi: Oxford University Press

Thapar, Romila (ed.). 2015. *The Public Intellectual in India*. New Delhi: Aleph

Tharoor, Shashi. 2018. *Why I Am a Hindu*. New Delhi: Aleph Book Company

Trivedi, Prashant K., Goli, Srinivas, Fahimuddin and Kumar, Surinder. 2016. 'Untouchability Exist among Muslims? Evidence from Uttar Pradesh'. *Economic and Political Weekly*, Vol. 51. No. 15. Pp. 32–36

Varshney, Ashutosh, 2022. 'India's Democratic Longevity and Its Troubled Trajectory'. In Masoud Tarek, and Mainwaring, Scott. (eds.). *Democracy in Hard Places*. New York: Oxford University Press.

Verma, Rahul, and Pranav Gupta. 2016. 'Facts and Fiction about How Muslims Vote in India: Evidence from Uttar Pradesh'. *Economic and Political Weekly*. Pp. 110–116

Waikar, Prashant. 2018. *Reading Islamophobia in Hindutva: An Analysis of Narendra Modi's Political Discourse. Islamophobia Studies Journal*. Vol. 4. No. 2 (Spring). Pp. 161–180

Wilkinson, Steven. 2004. *Votes and Violence: Electoral Competition and Communal Riots in India*. Cambridge: Cambridge University Press

Wright Jr, Theodore P. 1966. 'The effectiveness of Muslim representation in India.' *South Asian Politics and Religion*. 105. Pp. 43–54

Reports

Attitudes, Anxieties and Aspirations of India's Youth: Changing Patterns. 2017. New Delhi: CSDS–Lokniti KAS

Indian Youth: Aspiration and Vision for the Future. 2021. New Delhi: CSDS-Lokniti KAS

Religion in India: Tolerance and Segregation. 2021. https://www.pewforum.org/2021/06/29/religion-in-india-tolerance-and-segregation./ Accessed on 30 March 2022

Politics and Society between Elections. 2017–2019. https://www. lokniti.org/PoliticsandSocietybetweenElections. Accessed on 7 March 2022

Report of the National Commission for Religious and Linguistic Minorities. 2007. New Delhi: Government of India

Report of the National Commission to Review the Working of the Constitution. 2000. https://legalaffairs.gov.in/sites/default/ files/chapter%2011.pdf

The Prime's High-Level Committee on Social, Economic and Educational Status of the Muslim Community in India. 2007. Sachar Commission Report. Sachar Committee Recommendations-English.pdf (minorityaffairs.gov.in

The Report of the First Backward Classes Commission, 1951. New Delhi: Government of India

Evaluation of Prime Minister's New 15 Point Programme for Welfare of Minorities. New Delhi: Ministry of Minority Affairs

Notes

Introduction

1   'RPF Constable Chetan Singh accused of Killing Four remanded in Police Custody till August 7', Sonam Saigal, *The Hindu*, 1 August 2023, https://www.thehindu.com/news/cities/mumbai/rpf-constable-chetan-singh-accused-of-killing-four-remanded-in-police-custody-till-aug-7/article67145481.ece.

2   'RPF constable kills senior, 3 passengers on board Jaipur-Mumbai train; nabbed while trying to flee', Sagar Rajput, Sweety Adimulam and Avishek G. Dastidar, *Indian Express*, 6 August 2023, https://indianexpress.com/article/cities/mumbai/maharashtra-rpf-jawan-shoots-dead-four-persons-train-8868611/, accessed on 9 August 2023.

3   Cow Protection Legislation and Vigilante Violence in India, 2021.

4   The 'jihad chart' Sudhir Chaudhary based his entire show on? It's plagiarised, NL Team, 12 March 2020, https://www.newslaundry.com/2020/03/12/did-you-see-sudhir-chaudharys-nutty-jihad-chart-he-plagiarised-it, accessed on 9 August 2023.

5   The 'jihad chart' Sudhir Chaudhary based his entire show on? It's plagiarised, NL Team, 12 March 2020, https://www.newslaundry.com/2020/03/12/did-you-see-sudhir-chaudharys-nutty-jihad-chart-he-plagiarised-it, accessed on 9 August 2023.

6   Mahatma Gandhi on Sarvdharm Sambhav - YouTube, https://www.youtube.com/watch?v=VAqWj-Q0k_o&ab_channel=PrasarBharatiArchives, accessed on 9 August 2023.

7   Bhargava, 2017.

8   Waikar, 2018.

9   For a detailed discussion on this point see deSouza, Ahmed and Alam, 2019.

10 Prasad and Irfan Nooruddin, 2019.

11 For an excellent discussion on this point see, Jayal, 1994.

12 Kumar, 2013.

13 'RGI releases Census 2011 data on Population by Religious Communities', 25 August 2015, https://pib.gov.in/newsite/PrintRelease.aspx?relid=126326.

14 CSDS-Lokniti-National Election Studies (NES) 2019, CSDS Lokniti-Indian Youth: Aspiration and Vision for the Future, 2021 are two relevant examples in this regard. See: All India Post-Poll NES https://www.lokniti.org/media/PDF-upload/1579771857_30685900_download_report.pdf.

15 Imtiaz Ahmad, 1972.

16 It is worth noting that French philosopher Michel Foucault used the phrase 'history of their present' in his book *Discipline and Punish* (1979) in an interesting manner. Explaining this seemingly paradoxical idea, Foucault argues: 'I set out from a problem expressed in the terms current today and I try to work out its genealogy. Genealogy means that I begin my analysis from a question posed in the present.' Kritzman 1988. In another interview he further elaborates this point. He says: ' . . . the question that serves as my point of departure is: What are we, and what are we today? What is this moment that is ours? So . . . it is a history that takes the present as its point of departure.' Brion el al, 2014, p. 235. I find this formulation very useful and productive.

17 It is worth noting that M.S. Golwalkar, one of the leading RSS ideologues and the author of a famous book *Bunch of Thoughts* was not fully comfortable with the term 'Hindutva'. Golwalkar says: 'Veer Savarkarji wrote a beautiful book 'Hindutva' and Hindu Mahasabha based itself on that pure philosophy of Hindu Nationalism. But once, the Hindu Mahasabha passed a resolution that Congress should not give up its "nationalist" stand by holding talks with Muslim League but should ask Hindu Mahasabha to do that job! It only means that . . . Hindu Mahasabha represented the Hindu counterpart of the rabidly communal, anti-national Muslim League!' *Bunch of Thoughts* https://www.thehinducentre.com/multimedia/archive/02486/Bunch_of_Thoughts_2486072a.pdf, accessed on 19 October 2023.

18 'A Hindu . . . is he who looks upon the land that extends from Sindu to Sindu-from the Indus to the Seas, as the land of his forefathers—his Fatherland (Pitribhu), who inherits the blood of that race whose first discernible source could be traced to the Vedic Saptasindhus . . . who has inherited . . . common classical language Sanskrit and represented by a common history, a common literature, art and architecture, law and jurisprudence, rites and rituals, ceremonies and sacraments, fairs and festivals; and who above all, addresses this land, this Sindhusthan as his Holyland (Punyabhu), as the land of his prophets and seers, of his godmen and gurus, the land of piety and pilgrimage.' (Savarkar, 1969, pp. 115–116).

19 Ahmed, 2019, pp. 63–70. Chapter 2 also discusses this point in great detail.

20 I have tried to provide a historical analysis of this phenomenon in my book, *Siyasi Muslims* (2019). For details see Ahmed, 2019, Chapter 4.

21 'Religion in India: Tolerance and Segregation', https://www.pewresearch.org/religion/2021/06/29/religion-in-

india-tolerance-and-segregation/, accessed on 9 August 2023.

22 Talal Asad reminds us that 'faith is inseparable from the particularities of the temporal world and the traditions that inhabit it. If one is to understand one's own faith-as opposed to having it-or to understand the faith of another, one needs to deploy the relevant concept whose criteria of application must be public-in a language that inhabits this world.' (Asad, 2001, p. 212).

23 I find Ashutosh Varshney's argument very useful to elaborate this point. Varshney argues, 'India's record as an electoral democracy is far better than its record as a liberal democracy. Electoral vitality coexists with liberal deficits. This is in part due to a founding ambiguity in India's Constitution. The Constitution vigorously supports the idea of universal franchise, but by making citizen freedoms subject to considerations of public order, not simply national security, the Constitution has installed a weaker notion of civil liberties. The ruling governmental regimes have basically determined how liberally, or restrictively, the idea of civil liberties would be interpreted and executed. The courts have not been a consistently strong exponent of civil freedoms' (Varshney, 2022, p. 68).

Chapter 1: Muslimness and Intellectual Politics

1 An older version of this chapter was published in M.H. Illias (ed.). *Research in the Islamic Context Political and Methodological Reflections from South Asia, Indian Ocean and the Arab World.* Routledge: London and New York. 2023 Pp. 88–101. I am thankful to the editor for granting me the permission. The present chapter is fully revised and updated.

2 'Why I Protest as a Muslim', Irena Akbar, *Indian Express*, 3 January 2020, https://indianexpress.com/article/opinion/columns/why-i-protest-as-a-muslim-citizenship-act-lucknow-6197041/, accessed on 9 August 2023.

3 'Sharjeel Imam's AMU Speech Sparks Row; Assam Police Slaps Sedition', 25 January 2020, Nivedita Niranjankumar and Anmol Alphonso, Boom Live, https://www.boomlive.in/politics/sharjeel-imams-amu-speech-sparks-row-assam-police-slaps-sedition-6662, accessed on 9 August 2023.

4 'The Design behind Sharjeel', 4 February 2020, Organiser, https://organiser.org/2020/02/04/126458/bharat/the-design-behind-sharjeel/ accessed on 9 August 2023.

5 'No sole organiser of Shaheen Bagh: Protestors issue statement over Sharjeel Imam row', *India Today*, 25 January 2020, https://www.indiatoday.in/india/story/shaheen-bagh-sharjeel-imam-organiser-protest-assam-agitate-video-1640170-2020-01-25, accessed on 9 August 2023.

6 'Dr. Ghazala Jamil addresses at JNU in Solidarity with Sharjeel Imam', https://www.youtube.com/watch?v=lzH2RGS_oq8, accessed on 9 August 2023.

7 'Sharjeel ke Video ka sach aur urghoti BJP ki boli', https://www.youtube.com/watch?v=Ct8pPxKZQGs, accessed on 9 August 2023.

8 It is worth noting that the Constitution of India introduces the terms such as 'minority, Schedule Caste (SC)' and 'Scheduled Tribe (ST)' as secular administrative categories. However, this schema changed in the 1990s. In 1992, the National Commission for Minorities Act was passed, which led to the establishment of the National Commission for Minorities (NCM) in May 1993. Following this mandate, the Government of India notified five religious' communities: Muslims, Christians, Sikhs, Buddhists

and Zoroastrians (Parsis) as national religious minorities in October1993. This list was amended in 2014, when Jains were notified as a national minority. For a detailed discussion on this point, see DeSouza, Ahmed, Alam 2019.

9 Broadly speaking, Muslim appeasement refers to at least two aspects of politics with regard to Muslims: biased institutional apparatus and unfair political practices. I have discussed the conceptual contours of the idea of Muslim appeasement in my book *Siyasi Muslims*. I argue that Muslim appeasement is not a description of an objective, socio-political condition of Muslims. Rather, it is a *metaphor* of politics, which is invoked primarily to underline the privileged position of Muslims in India. See Ahmed, 2019, pp. 185–186.

10 For an excellent discussion on Muslim self-perceptions as Muslims in south Asian context, see Jaffery and Sen, 2015.

11 I intentionally do not wish to go into some of the stereotypical questions such as why most of the time Muslim researchers are either encouraged to work on Muslims or they themselves prefer to work on Muslims. Although I recognize the polemical values of such assertions, I would prefer to approach this question from a somewhat operational point of view of research.

12 Akeel Bilgrami's distinction between 'subjective' and 'objective' aspects of the concepts of identity is very useful to elaborate this point. Bilgrami rightly point out that 'which of these two aspects we emphasize in our study of the concept will be a matter of theoretical decision . . . This is to be expected . . . because our notion of identity gains so much of its interest from the fact that identities get mobilized in politics under conditions of oppression' Bilgrami, 2018, p. 166. Gerd Baumann's work is also relevant to make the distinction between self-perception and popular discourse on identities. See Bauman, 1996.

13 For a similar and elaborated discussion on this point see Sökefeld, 2001.

14 Ahmed, 2020.

15 Ahmed, 2016.

16 Jamiat Ulama-e-Hind's commissioned translation of the Quran was sent to some of the Hindi experts, including Kanhaiya Lal Mishr 'Prabhakar', for their approval so that an 'authentic' Hindi version could be produced. (Madani, 1991).

17 Thapar, 2015.

18 Ahmed, 2014, Chapter 3.

19 Ahmad 1972, p. 177.

20 Ahmed, 2014.

21 Ahmad, 1981, p. 18.

22 For an excellent discussion on this point, see, Kaviraj, 2013.

23 This political divide was deeply associated with the Ayodhya controversy. This legal dispute originated in the 19th century when it was claimed that the Babri Masjid—a sixteenth century mosque built by the first Mughal emperor Babar in the north Indian city of Ayodhya—was actually constructed on the site where Hindu God Lord Rama was born. In December 1949, the mosque was illegally occupied by a mob who mob installed the idols of Lord Ram in the mosque and transformed it into a temple. The mosque was taken over by the administration and was closed for both the communities. However, the idols were not removed from the mosque. A Hindu priest was officially appointed to worship these idols. This led to a series of legal cases for the ownership of the site. In 1986, a local court allowed the Hindus for unrestricted worship of these idols. The Hindu nationalist party, the BJP, officially launched a movement for constructing a Hindu temple on this site in 1987. The structure of the mosque was demolished by a Hindu mob

led by a few BJP leaders in 1992. The Supreme Court of India finally gave its verdict in favour of Hindus on a few technical grounds in 2019 (Civil Appeal Nos 10866-10867 of 2010, https://www.sci.gov.in/pdf/JUD_2.pdf accessed on 14 December 2023). For detailed discussion on this point, see Ahmed, 2014.

24 Hasan, 1997, page 227.

25 Hasan, 1997, page 320.

26 For a conceptual discussion on the idea of good Muslim and bad Muslims in Indian politics, see, Ahmed, 2019.

27 In an interview with us, Rajni Kothari elaborates this point. He said: 'the task of intellectuals is not limited to the study of the critical role played by politics at various levels; they also have to develop various critiques of existing politics. I also suggest that intellectuals must intervene in the political process by linking critical ideas to political debates. In this framework, intellectual intervention finds a legitimate space. I also believe that there should be a space for criticism and self-criticism in our thinking. If we close the possibility of criticism, the gap between ideas and processes will increase. It will restrict our role as intellectuals in society.' (Ahmed, Vijaisri, Dubey, 2012)

28 Ali, 2002, p. 616.

29 DeSouza, 2015, p. 79.

30 For a detailed discussion on this point, see, Ahmed, 2012.

31 Gandhi writes: '. . . I am not at all concerned with appearing to be consistent . . . therefore, when anybody finds any inconsistency between any two writings of mine, if he has still faith in my sanity, he would do well to choose the later of the two on the same subject.' (Gandhi, 1938, p. 2)

32 For a detailed discussion on the idea of intellectual politics in the Indian context, see Ahmed, 2013

Chapter 2: What is New in New India?

1   An earlier version of this argument was published as 'New India, Hindutva Constitutionalism, and Muslim Political Attitudes', *Studies in Indian Politics*, Vol 10, No. 1 https://journals.sagepub.com/doi/pdf/10.1177/23210230221082833. 2022. Pp 1–17. I am thankful to editor for granting me the permission.

2   'A New India By 2022, Vows PM Modi On Independence Day: 10 Points', NDTV, 15 August 2017, https://www.ndtv.com/india-news/india-stands-with-those-affected-by-gorakhpur-tragedy-says-pm-narendra-modi-1737728, accessed on 9 August 2022.

3   'Full Transcript of Indian Prime Minister Narendra Modi's Independence Day Speech', *Time*, 15 August 2017, https://time.com/4901564/narendra-modi-india-70-independence-day-speech/, accessed on 9 August 2022.

4   'PM Narendra Modi leading to develop a "New India"', Kamal Sandesh, 17 September 2018, http://www.kamalsandesh.org/pm-narendra-modi-leading-develop-new-india/, accessed on 9 August 2022.

5   This document notes: 'The "Strategy for New India @ 75" captures three key messages from the Prime Minister. First, development must become a mass movement, in which every Indian recognizes her role and also experiences the tangible benefits accruing to her in the form of better ease of living. . . . Second, development strategy should help achieve broad-based economic growth to ensure balanced development across all regions and states and across sectors. Third, the strategy when implemented, will bridge the gap between public and private sector performance. The Prime Minister has focused on putting in place a 'development state' in place of the 'soft state' that this government had

inherited". Strategy New India@75, https://www.niti.gov.in/the-strategy-for-new-india, accessed on 9 August 2022.

6   'PM Narendra Modi launches #IAmNewIndia, 'a pledge to build a new India on NaMo app', *Times of India,* 12 March 2017, https://timesofindia.indiatimes.com/india/pm-narendra-modi-launches-iamnewindia-a-pledge-to-build-a-new-india-on-namo-app/articleshow/57605914.cms, accessed on 17 October 2023.

7   'After poll win, PM Narendra Modi asks people to pledge to create "new India" by 2022', *Economic Times,* 12 March 2017, https://economictimes.indiatimes.com/news/politics-and-nation/after-poll-win-pm-narendra-modi-asks-people-to-pledge-to-create-new-india-by-2022/articleshow/57607764.cms?from=mdr, accessed on 16 August 2023.

8   'New India is about the voice of each and every of 130 crore Indians', 30 August 2019, https://www.narendramodi.in/text-of-pm-s-address-at-malayala-manorama-news-conclave-2019--546229, accessed on 9 August 2022.

9   There is a considerable literature on various aspects of Indian constitutionalism. *The Politics and Ethics of Indian Constitution* (see Bhargava, 2008) was the first systematic attempt in this regard. This edited volume tries to unpack various theoretical-political aspects of the Indian Constitution. In recent years, scholars have expanded the scope this discussion in a significant way. The contributions of Uday S. Mehta, Ornit Shani, Rohit De, and Madhav Khosla are very relevant in this regard. Madhav Khosla's explanation of the idea of constitution in the Indian context is useful to understand the evolving nature of Indian constitutionalism. (Khosla, 2020, pp. 28–72)

10 Rohit De introduces us to the popular reception of Indian constitutionalism. Exploring 'a new genealogy of Indian

constitutionalism' that emerges from the everydayness of people's life, he unpacks the process by which the Constitution emerged as a realm of possibilities for citizens. (De, 2018, pp. 30–31)

11 In a landmark judgement, the Supreme Court of India conceptualized the term 'Hindutva' as a way of life (AIR 1996 SC, 1113). Although the Court criticized the use of any direct reference to any religion in electoral campaigns, it did not find the use of term Hindutva objectionable. This verdict encouraged the Hindu nationalist groups to describe their politics as *expressions of Hindutva*. For an elaborated discussion on this point, especially the BJP's changing attitude on Hindutva, see Ahmed, 2019, pp. 65–73.

12 For detailed discussion on Jan Sangh/BJP's relationship with the Constitution, see Ahmed, 2020.

13 'Sab ka Saath Sab ka Vikas Collective Efforts Inclusive Growth', 9 May 2014, https://www.narendramodi.in/sabka-saath-sabkavikas-collective-efforts-inclusive-growth-31590, accessed on 9 August 2022.

14 Our Constitution has kept us united: PM, 26 November 2017, https://www.narendramodi.in/excerpts-of-pm-s-address-at-the-valedictory-function-of-national-law-day-2017--537951, accessed on 9 August 2022.

15 In his presidential address of 2004, L.K. Advani said: 'I am saddened that from being a description of the core of our nationhood, Hindutva has been misrepresented to denote a political approach. Hindutva is a sentiment; it is neither an electoral slogan nor should it be confused with religion.' http://library.bjp.org/jspui/bitstream/123456789/247/1/Lal%20Krishna%20Advani.pdf, accessed on 9 August 2022.

16 This is the original Hindi text of the speech: इन दिनों उन्होंने अभी चुनाव में बताइए . . . कह रहे हैं कि मोदी को हिंदू का कोई ज्ञान ही नहीं है। अरे भाई मोदी को ज्ञान

है या नहीं है, क्या राजस्थान में इसके मुद्दे पर वोट डालना है क्या . . . । राजस्थान को बिजली, सड़क, पानी के लिए वोट चाहिए कि मोदी को हिंदू का ज्ञान है कि नहीं है, उस पर वोट चाहिए। वो इसकी बात कर रहे हैं, मैं तो समझ नहीं पा रहा हूं भाई। हां मैं ये बात जरूर कहूंगा, हजारों साल पुरानी ये संस्कृति है, ये परंपरा है। ऋषियों, मुनियों की तपस्या से निकला हुआ ये ज्ञान का भंडार है। हर युग में, हर कसौटी से खरा उतरा हुआ ये हिंदुत्व एक विपुल विरासत है। और ये हिंदुत्व, ये हिंदू का ज्ञान इतना अगाध है, इतना अगाध है, इतना विशाल, इतना चिर पुरातन है, इतना चिरंजीव है, ये इतना हिमालय से भी ऊंचा है, समंदर से भी गहरा है। ऋषि, मुनियों ने भी कभी दावा नहीं किया उन्हें हिंदू और हिंदुत्व का पूरा ज्ञान है। किसी ने नहीं किया, ये इतना विशाल है कि कोटि-कोटि जन्मों के बावजूद भी इस पूरे ज्ञान को समेटना इंसान के बस की बात नहीं है। ये तो एक छोटा कामदार है। मोदी एक ऐसा कामदार है, मैं इस अगाध ज्ञान का भंडार मेरे पास है, ऐसा दावा कभी नहीं कर सकता हूं। Text of PM Modi's Speech at Jodhpur, Rajasthan, https://www.narendramodi.in/text-of-pm-modi-s-speech-at-jodhpur-rajasthan-542576, 3 December 2018, accessed on 9 August 2022.

17 1998 election manifesto of the BJP says: 'Cultural heritage which is central to all regions, religions and languages, is a civilizational identity and constitutes the cultural nationalism of India which is the core of Hindutva', http://library.bjp.org/jspui/bitstream/123456789/241/1/BJP%20ELECTION%20MANIFESTO%201998.pdf, accessed on 9 August 2022. The BJP no longer uses the term Hindutva to describe its political philosophy. In fact, one finds an interesting division of labor between the BJP and the RSS. In post-2014, the RSS has worked hard to offer a workable conceptualization of the term Hindutva. For an elaborated on this point, see, Ahmed, 2019, Chapter 4.

18 Narendra Modi says: ' . . . today the Constitution Day has posed an important question to us. As the members of a family, have we been following those values which have been expected of us by our guardian, by our Constitution? Have we been working to cooperate with each other to strengthen each other like the members of a family? . . . every institution that obtains power from constitution will have to channelize its energy and will have to devote itself only for one purpose to realize the dream of a New India'. Our Constitution has kept us united: PM Modi (narendramodi. in), accessed on 9 August 2023.

19 According to the RSS chief, Mohan Bhagwat: 'Our constitution (is) . . . based on the understanding of the "bharatiya" ethos of our founding fathers, but many of the laws that we are still using are based on the foreign sources and that laws were made as per their thinking . . . seven decades have passed since our independence . . . this is something we must address,' RSS chief Mohan Bhagwat says there is need to develop legal system based on 'ethos of society, as quoted on Firstpost, https://www.firstpost.com/india/rss-chief-mohan-bhagwat-says-there-is-need-to-develop-legal-system-based-on-ethos-of-society-4029775.html, 10 September 2017, accessed on 9 August 2023.

20 'Today, we have to live for the nation and build India our freedom fighters dreamt of: PM Modi', 25 June 2019, https://www.narendramodi.in/text-of-prime-minister-narendra-modi-s-reply-to-the-motion-of-thanks-on-the-president-s-address-in-the-lok-sabha-545486/, accessed on 9 August 2023.

21 The idea of Hindu victimhood is based on a strong assumption that Hindus, despite being a majority in India, face discrimination and exploitation. See Tripathi, Kumar, Tripathi, 2019.

22 'PIL In SC For Granting Minority Status To Hindus In 8 States [Read Petition]', Live Law, https://www.livelaw. in/pil-sc-granting-minority-status-hindus-8-states-read-petition, 31 October 2017, accessed on 9 August 2023.

23 For a historical discussion on this point see Ahmed, 2020.

24 'A new dawn in Jammu & Kashmir and Ladakh', Kamal Sandesh,http://www.kamalsandesh.org/new-dawn-jammu-kashmir-ladakh/, 17 August 2019, accessed on 9 August 2023.

25 https://www.ugc.ac.in/ugc_notices.aspx?id=NDYxNQ==, accessed on 9 August 2023.

26 'Celebration of the Constitution Day ICMR', ICMR 21 November 2022, https://main.icmr.nic.in/sites/default/files/Circulars_front/Celebration_of_Constitution_Day_on_26th_Nov_2022.pdf

27 'India is Mother of Democracy: PM Modi During Mann ki Baat', 29 January 2023, https://www.narendramodi.in/pm-modi-s-mann-ki-baat-2023-january-567430, accessed on 9 August 2023.

28 'Distorted Histories and Unconstitutional Autocracy in the "Mother of Democracy"', Rajesh Venkatasubramaniam, Wire, 19 November 2022, https://thewire.in/communalism/distorted-histories-inmother-of-democracy; Sumit Guha, 2023 Was India the Mother of Democracy? https://www.theindiaforum.in/history/was-india-mother-democracy accessed on 14 December 2023.

29 'Distorted Histories and Unconstitutional Autocracy in the "Mother of Democracy"', Rajesh Venkatasubramaniam, Wire, 19 November 2022, https://thewire.in/communalism/distorted-histories-inmother-of-democracy

30 Celebration of the Constitution Day ICMR', ICMR, 21 November 2022, https://main.icmr.nic.in/sites/default/files/Circulars_front/Celebration_of_Constitution_Day_on_26th_Nov_2022.pdf.

31 'Playing against BJP on Congress prepared pitch due to yatra', *The Hindu*, 18 December 2022, https://www. thehindu.com/news/national/playing-against-bjp-on-congress-prepared-pitch-due-to-yatra-jairam-ramesh/article66277429.ece, accessed on 9 August 2023.

32 The Article 4 of the BJP's Party Constitution adheres to the idea of positive secularism, https://www.bjp.org/files/2020-01/constitution_eng_jan_10_2013%20%281%29.pdf accessed on 14 December 2023.

33 National Democrats Democratic Socialists & National Socialists, http://deendayalupadhyay.org/national.html, accessed on 9 August 2023.

34 'Congress practises pseudo-secularism: Advani', 21 April 2009, *India Today*, https://www.indiatoday.in/elections-north/story/congress-practises-pseudo-secularism-advani-45170-2009-04-20, accessed on 14 December 2023.

35 Election Manifesto 1999, https://library.bjp.org/jspui/bitstream/123456789/242/1/BJP%20ELECTION%20MANIFESTO%201999.pdf, accessed on 9 August 2023.

36 'Everything that harms and affect development of the country have to be kept away: PM', 16 July 2022, https://www.narendramodi.in/text-of-prime-minister-narendra-modi-s-address-at-inauguration-of-bundelkhand-expressway-at-jalaun-in-uttar-pradesh-563189, accessed on 9 August 2023.

37 'PM Modi May Decry "Revdi Culture" – But it Still Runs Our Political Economy', Arun Kumar, Wire, 25 July 2022, https://thewire.in/political-economy/narendra-modi-revdi-culture-political-economy, accessed on 14 December 2023.

38 'From freebies to welfare', N.K. Singh, *Indian Express*, 28 July 2022, https://indianexpress.com/article/opinion/columns/pm-modis-remarks-on-revdi-culture-should-be-

heeded-by-those-promising-imprudent-unsustainable-subsidies-8055674/, accessed on 9 August 2023.

39 'Everything that harms and affect development of the country have to be kept away: PM', 16 July 2022, https://www.narendramodi.in/text-of-prime-minister-narendra-modi-s-address-at-inauguration-of-bundelkhand-expressway-at-jalaun-in-uttar-pradesh-563189, accessed on 9 August 2023.

40 Amit Shah interview: 'Anger comes out when people do not have confidence in leadership . . . But people have confidence in PM Modi', Liz Mathew, P. Vaidyanathan Iyer, *Indian Express*, 1 March 2022, https://indianexpress.com/elections/amit-shah-interview-uttar-pradesh-elections-pm-modi-bjp-7794992/, accessed on 9 August 2023.

41 'Everything that harms and affect development of the country have to be kept away: PM', 16 July 2022, https://www.narendramodi.in/text-of-prime-minister-narendra-modi-s-address-at-inauguration-of-bundelkhand-expressway-at-jalaun-in-uttar-pradesh-563189, accessed on 9 August 2023.

42 'Everything that harms and affect development of the country have to be kept away: PM', 16 July 2022, https://www.narendramodi.in/text-of-prime-minister-narendra-modi-s-address-at-inauguration-of-bundelkhand-expressway-at-jalaun-in-uttar-pradesh-563189, accessed on 9 August 2023.

43 'Everything that harms and affect development of the country have to be kept away: PM', 16 July 2022, https://www.narendramodi.in/text-of-prime-minister-narendra-modi-s-address-at-inauguration-of-bundelkhand-expressway-at-jalaun-in-uttar-pradesh-563189, accessed on 9 August 2023

Chapter 3: New India and the Muslim Historical

1   'PM Modi's Independence Day Speech Is High on Lofty Rhetoric but Devoid of Plan of Action', Akash Satyawali, Wire, 15 August 2023, https://thewire.in/politics/narendra-modi-independence-day-speech-rhetoric-plan accessed on 14 December 2023.

2   'PM Narendra Modi Independence Day speech full text', *Indian Express*, 15 August 2023, https://indianexpress.com/article/india/prime-minister-narendra-modi-independence-day-speech-2023-full-text-8893141/, accessed on 16 August 2023.

3   Hasan, 2002.

4   PM Narendra Modi Independence Day speech full text, *Indian Express*, https://indianexpress.com/article/india/prime-minister-narendra-modi-independence-day-speech-2023-full-text-8893141/ accseed on 14 December 2023.

5   Shashi Tharoor, 2018.

6   Pavan K. Varma, 1989, *Ghalib: The Man, The Times*, New Delhi: Penguin Books.

7   Varma, 2021, p. 4.

8   Varma, 2021, p. 189.

9   Tharoor, 208, p. 106.

10 Varma, 2021, p. 201.

11 'Rethinking Meo Identity', Shail Mayaram, https://read.dukeupress.edu/cssaame/article-abstract/17/2/35/437/Rethinking-Meo-Identity-Cultural-Faultline?redirectedFrom=fulltext, accessed on 9 August 2023.

12 Varma, 2021, p. 288.

13 Parveen, 2021.

14 Tharoor writes, 'As a Hindu and an Indian, I would argue that the whole point about India is the rejection of the idea that religion should be a determinant of nationhood.

Our nationalist leaders did not jump to the conclusion that a Partition-formed Muslim state dictated an equivalent one for Hindus. To accept the idea of India you have to spurn the logic that divided the country in 1947. Your Indianness has nothing to do with which god you choose to worship, or not. We are not going to reduce ourselves to a **Hindu Pakistan**.' (Tharoor, 2018, p. 262).

15 Varma, pp. 305–310.

16 Transparency on demolition of National Archives of India and Transfer of its holdings, 17 May 2021, https://docs.google.com/forms/d/1nVmGjN3n67EGZR35Ztwz235-JNMae-iux1-863wxzes/viewform?gxids=7628&edit_requested=true, accessed on 9 August 2023.

17 'Why uprooting the National Archives of India is bad news for Indian history', Swapna Kona Nayudu, *Indian Express*, 23 May 2021, https://indianexpress.com/article/opinion/why-uprooting-the-national-archives-of-india-is-bad-news-for-indian-history-7326748/, accessed on 9 August 2023.

18 Sharma, R. S., Ali, M. Athar, Jha, D. N. and Bhan, Suraj, 1991, *Babari Mosque or Rama's Birth Place? Historians' Report to the Indian Nation*, Lucknow: Babri Masjid Action Committee (UP).

19 'Historians' report on Babri mosque mere "opinion": SC', Dhananjay Mahapatra, *Times of India*, 18 September 2019, https://timesofindia.indiatimes.com/india/historians-report-on-babri-mosque-mere-opinion-sc/articleshow/71176583.cms, accessed on 9 August 2023. It is also to be noted that the final verdict made an important comment about the Report. It says: 'The inferences which have been drawn by the historians in regard to the faith and belief of the Hindus in the birth-place of Lord Ram constitute their opinion. Evidence having been led in the suits, this Court cannot

rest a finding of fact on the report of the historians and must evaluate the entirety of the evidence.' (Civil Appeal Nos 10866–10867 of 2010)

20 'We want to make India a hub of heritage tourism: PM Modi', 11 January 2020, https://www.narendramodi. in/text-of-pm-s-address-at-the-dedication-of-four-refurbished-heritage-buildings-in-kolkata-to-the-nation-547949, accessed on 9 August 2023.

21 'Our history books need rewriting', Sanjeev Sanyal http:// www.sanjeevsanyal.com/home/article_detail/63, accessed on 9 August 2023

22 'The four reasons why Indian liberals are a fast-disappearing species', Chetan Bhagat, 8 November 2020, http://www. chetanbhagat.com/columns/the-four-reasons-why-indian-liberals-are-a-fast-disappearing-species/, accessed on 9 August 2023

23 *Selected Works of Jawaharlal Nehru* (SWJN), 1972. p. 504 (File no. 40(60)/49-PMS) dated 26 February 1949).

24 SWJN 1972, p. 504 (Note to Education Minister 26 February 1949).

25 *Discovery of India*, Jawaharlal Nehru, http://library. bjp.org:8080/jspui/bitstream/123456789/277/1/The-Discovery-Of-India-Jawaharlal-Nehru.pdf, accessed on 9 August 2023.

26 Kaviraj, 2010, pp. 39–41.

27 Prakash, 1990, Nandy el al, 1995, Bhattacharya 2008, Eaton 2000, Gopal, 1990

28 Section 6 of the CAA 2019 says: 'In the Third Schedule to the principal Act, in clause (d), the following proviso shall be inserted, namely:— Provided that for the person belonging to Hindu, Sikh, Buddhist, Jain, Parsi or Christian community in Afghanistan, Bangladesh or Pakistan, the aggregate period of residence or service of Government in

India as required under this clause shall be read as "not less than five years" in place of "not less than eleven years".'

29   This emerging form of Muslim political attitude is discussed systematically in Chapter 8.

Chapter 4: New India and the Muslim Cultural

1   Maurice, Thomas 1794, *Indian Antiquities: Or Dissertations relative to the Ancient Geography Divisions, the Pure System of Primeval Theology, the Grand Code of Civil Laws, the Original Form of Government, and the Various and Profound Literature of Hindostan*, (7 Volumes), London: C& W Galbin.

2   I have tried to offer a historical overview of this paradoxical process in my book, *Muslim Political Discourse in Postcolonial India: Monuments, Memory and Contestations* (2014), https://*www*.routledge.com/Muslim-Political-Discourse-in-*Postcolonial*-India-Monuments-Memory-Contestation/Ahmed/p/book/9780367176884.

3   Goradia, 2002.

4   'Indians Built Taj, Nothing Else Matters, Says Yogi Adityanath: 10 Facts', NDTV, 26 October 2017, https://www.ndtv.com/india-news/yogi-adityanath-visits-taj-mahal-today-to-make-a-point-10-points-1767223, accessed on 17 August 2023.

5   'Dara Shikoh Central to RSS "Assimilation" Project', Vasudha Venugopal, *Economic Times*, 25 June 2022, https://economictimes.indiatimes.com/news/politics-and-nation/shikoh-central-to-rss-assimilation-project/articleshow/92443897.cms?from=mdr, accessed on 17 October 2023.

6   'Sai Baba never claimed he is God; everybody free to choose whom to worship: RSS', *Financial Express*, 1 November 2015, https://www.financialexpress.com/india-news/sai-

baba-never-claimed-he-is-god-everybody-free-to-choose-whom-to-worship-rss/159714/, accessed on 17 August 2023.

7   In the Court of Civil Sr. Div. Judge Varanasi, https://images.assettype.com/barandbench/2021-02/a85729d4-ccd3-42b8-a7b0-b8106c727b25/1_Suit__1_.pdf, accessed on 17 August 2023.

8   The Place of Worship (Special Provisions Act 1991), https://www.mha.gov.in/sites/default/files/PlaceWorshipAct1991.pdf.

9   For detailed discussion on this point the Chapter 5 of my book, *Muslim Political Discourse in Postcolonial India: Monuments, Memory and Contestations* (2014), https://www.routledge.com/Muslim-Political-Discourse-in-Postcolonial-India-Monuments-Memory-Contestation/Ahmed/p/book/9780367176884, accessed on 17 August 2023.

10 For a detailed discussion on this point see Ahmed, 2014.

11 'Demolish Aurangzeb's tomb, MNS tells CM Thackeray; police deployed at site', Vallabh Ozarkar, *Indian Express*, 18 May 2022, https://indianexpress.com/article/cities/mumbai/demolish-aurangzebs-tomb-mns-tells-chief-minister-uddhav-thackeray/, accessed on 17 August 2023.

12 'Under Muslim rule, India was the richest country with 27% of world GDP: Shashi Tharoor', Siasat, 22 October 2017, https://archive.siasat.com/news/muslim-rule-india-richest-country-27-world-gdp-shashi-tharoor-1245760/.

13 'Hali's Musaddas', https://franpritchett.com/00urdu/hali/musaddas/index.html, accessed on 17 August 2023.

14 Syed Sharifuddin Pirzada (ed.), *Foundations of Pakistan: All India Muslim League Documents: 1906-1947*, National Publishing House Limited, Karachi, 1969, Vol. I, p. 44.

15 http://www.allamaiqbal.com/poet/prose/english/stray.pdf, p. 47, accessed on 17 August 2023.

16 'Maulana Abul Kalam Azad', Sarmad Shaheed in Sayeda Saiyidain Hameed, *The Rubbiyat of Sarmad,* Indian Council for Cultural Relations, New Delhi, pp. 34–42.

17 Alamgir https://www.rekhta.org/ebooks/detail/aalamgir-part-002-sadiq-hussain-saradhanvi-ebooks.

18 'Why it's wrong to say that Hinduism is a product of colonialism', Pratap Bhanu Mehta, *Indian Express*, 11 October 2022, https://indianexpress.com/article/opinion/columns/why-its-wrong-to-say-that-hinduism-is-a-product-of-colonialism-8203006/, accessed on 17 August 2023.

19 Savarkar, 1969.

20 'The Imaginary Institution of India', Sudipta Kaviraj, https://www.cscsarchive.org/dataarchive/otherfiles/PhD0010004/file, accessed on 17 August 2023.

Chapter 5: New India and the Muslim Religious

1 The argument presented in this chapter is based on my essay *Muslim Imagnations of Islam* published in Amir Ullah Khan and Nahia Hussain (eds.), 2023, *New Challenges for Indian Muslims: Beyond Citizenship Concerns.* Hyderabad: CDPP. Pp. 211–228. I am grateful to the editor for the permission.

2 There is a considerable literature on the impact of 9/11 and war on terror on the religious and political orientations of Muslims in the Arab world. For an excellent discussion, El Kurd, 2018.

3 There is a wide-spread acceptability of the Hindutva discourse even among the non-BJP public intellectuals and commentators. We have already discussed Pavan K. Varma's book, *The Great Hindu Civilization: Achievement, Neglect, Bias and the Way Forward* in the third chapter of this book. See Varma, 2021.

4   Ahmed, 2016, p. 6.

5   For a broad overview of the term *Islamophobia* see, Bleich, 2012.

6   For an elaborated discussion on various problematic representations of Muslim identity in postcolonial India, see Ahmed, 2019.

7   "'Wherever Muslims Live . . .': Text of Vajpayee's Controversial Goa Speech, April 2002'", 17 August 2018, https://thewire.in/preview/280293, accessed on 9 August 2023.

8   Interview of Prime Minister Dr. Manmohan Singh with CNN, 20 July 2005, https://www.mea.gov.in/interviews.htm?dtl/4535/Interview+of+Prime+Minister+Dr+Manmohan+Singh+with+CNN, accessed on 9 August 2023.

9   For an overview of media discourse on this issue, See Bajpai, 2021.

10   Levesque, 2020.

11   The report is based on interview of 29,999 Indian adults (including 22,975 who identify as Hindu, 3336 who identify as Muslim, 1782 who identify as Sikh, 1011 who identify as Christian, 719 who identify as Buddhist, 109 who identify as Jain and sixty-seven who identify as belonging to another religion or as religiously unaffiliated). Interviews for this nationally representative survey were conducted face-to-face from November 2019 to 23 March 2020. The questionnaire was developed in English and translated into sixteen languages, independently verified by professional linguists with native proficiency in regional dialects. See: https://www.pewresearch.org/religion/2021/06/29/religion-in-india-tolerance-and-segregation/.

12   A section of commentators rejected the Pew Survey. They argue that it has failed to capture the everyday form of Hindutva communalism and its impact on Muslim

psyche. The Report is juxtaposed with a few experience-based accounts of Muslim individuals to draw a pessimistic conclusion that nothing has left for Muslims in India. This strange comparison between *experience-based individual anecdotes of religious discrimination* and the *Survey findings based on structured questionnaire* is extremely misleading. The survey findings offer us a big picture of Muslim presence, while the individual stories and anecdotes introduce us to the complex everyday Muslim encounters with communalism. Both are valid. It is, thus, necessary to read the *macro analysis* of Muslim imagination in relation to individual *micro level* episodes of religious discrimination. Mukul Kesavan, *Telegraph*, 11 July 2021, https://www.telegraphindia.com/opinion/second-class-bogie-indias-muslim-passengers/cid/1821972, accessed 9 August 2023.

13 Journalist Mohammad Ali's recently published essay confirms this finding. 'The Scream', Mohammad Ali, July 2021, https://thebaffler.com/salvos/the-scream-ali, accessed 9 August 2023. Also see 'Second class Bogie', Mukul Kesavan, *Telegraph*, 11 July 2021, https://www.telegraphindia.com/opinion/second-class-bogie-indias-muslim-passengers/cid/1821972, accessed 9 August 2023.

14 For a detailed analysis see, Ahmed, 2021.

15 Various recent reports on Muslim aspirations, including a detailed study by Fatima Khan is very relevant to underline this point. See 'Not cows to be milked', Fatima Khan, Print, 7 April 2021 https://theprint.in/politics/not-cows-to-be-milked-muslims-in-bengal-kerala-assam-are-now-assertive-want-recognition/635205/, accessed 9 August 2023.

16 For interesting analysis of everyday Islamic religiosity, see Menon 2021.

17 'Religion in India: Tolerance and Segregation', https://www.pewresearch.org/religion/2021/06/29/religion-in-india-tolerance-and-segregation/.

18 This report is based on a representative sample of 6226 young respondents (aged between fifteen to thirty-four years) and it covers eighteen states.

19 For a detailed analysis of 2016 survey, See the CSDS-Lokniti Report, *Attitudes, Anxieties and Aspirations of India's Youth: Changing Patterns, 2017.*

20 For an excellent discussion on this point see Salam, 2020.

Chapter 6: New India and the Muslim Liberals

1 'Naseeruddin Shah's message to those celebrating Taliban's return', https://www.youtube. com/watch?v=blSqB61JNJk&t=3s&ab_channel=IndianExpressOnline, accessed on 18 August 2023.

2 'Naseeruddin Shah shares video message for those "celebrating Taliban's return", watch', *Indian Express,* 3 September 2021, https://indianexpress.com/article/entertainment/bollywood/naseeruddin-shah-shares-video-message-for-those-celebrating-talibans-return-watch-7483716/, accessed on 18 August 2023.

3 For a detailed analysis of Muslim political participation based on CSDS surveys see Ahmed 2019.

4 Bhargava, 2009.

5 'Javed Akhtar calls himself "equal opportunity atheist who is against all faiths" after offending both sides', *Hindustan Times,* 13 June 2020, https://www.hindustantimes.com/bollywood/javed-akhtar-calls-himself-equal-opportunity-atheist-who-is-against-all-faiths-after-offending-both-sides/story-tqFPdtO3nXs03lWzuqHQWI.html, accessed on 18 August 2023.

6   Idea Of Taliban Can't Appeal To Any Indian, Says
    Javed Akhtar: Highlights, https://www.ndtv.com/india- news/
    javed-akhtar-speaks-out-against-taliban-sympathisers-
    highlights-2528675

7   'Where Are Those Shouting in Defence of Triple Talaq,
    Asks Javed Akhtar as Taliban Ask Working Women to
    Stay Home', News18, 20 September 2021, https://www.
    news18.com/news/india/where-are-those-shouting-in-
    defence-of-triple-talaq-asks-javed-akhtar-as-taliban-ask-
    working-women-to-stay-home-4222190.html,   accessed
    on 18 August 2023.

8   Opposed to Muslim fundamentalists and Hindu extremism:
    Javed Akhtar, *Indian Express*, 20 September 2021, https://
    indianexpress.com/article/cities/mumbai/opposed-to-
    muslim-fundamentalists-and-hindu-extremism-javed-
    akhtar-7510220/, accessed on 18 August 2023.

9   'Congress practises pseudo-secularism: Advani', *India Today*,
    https://www.indiatoday.in/elections-north/story/congress-
    practises-pseudo-secularism-advani-45170-2009-04-20
    accessed on 14 December 2023.

10 'Minority report for the BJP', Hilal Ahmed, *Indian Express*,
    15   September   2017,   https://indianexpress.com/article/
    opinion/columns/minority-report-for-the-bjp-up-gujarat-
    muslim-4655830/, accessed on 18 August 2023.

11 'Union Minister Najma Heptullah's Stand on Muslim
    Reservation Upsets Minority Community',   Saurabh
    Gupta, NDTV, 3 January 2015, https://www.ndtv.com/
    india-news/union-minister-najma-heptullahs-stand-on-
    muslim-reservation-upsets-minority-community-722136,
    accessed on 18 August 2023.

12 'Under PM Narendra Modi, India is no country
    for appeasement and victim card politics anymore',
    Shehzad Poonawala, *Indian Express*, 24 September 2020,

https://indianexpress.com/article/opinion/columns/no-country-for-appeasement-6606700/, accessed on 18 August 2023.

13 'BJP's Shazia Ilmi writes on Bilkis Bano remission: My personal sense of justice feels betrayed', Shazia Ilmi, *Indian Express*, 10 September 2022, https://indianexpress.com/article/opinion/columns/bjp-shazia-ilmi-writes-bilkis-bano-remission-sense-justice-feels-betrayed-8141620/, accessed on 18 August 2023.

14 'VHP hits back at Shazia Ilmi: BJP must come clean on Bilkis convicts issue', Pravesh Kumar Choudhary, *Indian Express*, 10 September 2022, https://indianexpress.com/article/opinion/columns/pravesh-kumar-choudhry-writes-vhp-shazia-ilmi-bjp-bilkis-convicts-issue-8142817/, accessed on 18 August 2023.

15 Suroor, Hasan, 2019, *Who Killed Liberal Islam*, New Delhi: Rupa.

16 Indian Muslim scholars' support for Turkey's Erdogan is alarming, Mohammad Behzad Fatmi, DailyO, 16 August 2016, https://www.dailyo.in/politics/erdogan-turkey-coup-fethullah-gulen-shahi-imam-salman-hussaini-nadvi-morsi-ottoman-caliphate-osama-12434, accessed on 18 August 2023.

17 For an excellent analysis see Anderson, 2015.

Chapter 7: New India and the Muslim Social

1 'BJP's Pasmanda Move Pushes Muslim Politics To A New Moment', *Outlook*, https://www.outlookindia.com/national/bjp-s-pasmanda-move-pushes-muslim-politics-to-a-new-moment-news-217046.

2 'The Hindu Right's ploy to win over Pasmanda Muslims, Shaikh Mujibur Rehman', *The Hindu*, https://www.

thehindu.com/opinion/op-ed/the-hindu-rights-ploy-to-win-over-pasmanda-muslims/article66366675.ece.

3   Ansari, 1960.

4   Ansari, Ali Anwar, 2023.

5   'Muslim vote: How BJP trumped Congress', *Economic Times*, https://economictimes.indiatimes.com/news/elections/lok-sabha/muslim-vote-how-bjp-trumped-congress/articleshow/68592698.cms?utm_source=contentofinterest&utm_medium=text&utm_campaign=cppst.

6   Ahmad, 1972.

7   Ansari notes, 'Although, it has ·been generally established that the caste system is a Hindu phenomenon . . . many non-Hindu communities of India, having their origin either directly in India or elsewhere, have also acquired this phenomenon as the basis of their social structures. It is interesting from an ethnological viewpoint to study how peoples of other creeds have, in the course of time, adopted this system of social stratification although their creeds and doctrines are basically opposed to any such distinctions as 'castes'. (Ansari, 1960, p. 1)

8   For an elaborated discussion on this point, see Ahmad, 2009.

9   Mattison Mines offers us a different reading of social stratification among Muslims. Mines argues: ' . . . It is only when Muslims form corporate groups which interact in the Hindu caste system-just as any other Hindu caste does-that we can speak of Muslim caste in the same sense as Hindu caste. Where this degree of integration is absent, behavior and ideology clearly distinguish Muslim stratification from Hindu caste stratification. Because of these socially important distinctions particular care must be taken when using the term "caste" to describe Muslim

social stratification. Unless the groups being discussed are actually comparable to Hindu castes, in terms of both behavior and accompanying ideology, a better term would be "subdivision." This term has the advantage of not implying the existence of an integrated system of social ranking, nor the rigidity of the Hindu system of caste ranking (Mines, 1972, p. 348)

10 Ahmad, 1967, p. 890.

11 I use the term *Dalit Muslims* following the suggestion given by Satish Deshpande in this regard. He uses this term to 'refer to those Muslims . . . who occupy—or claim to occupy, or are believed to occupy—a position in society comparable to that of the officially designated SCs belonging to the Hindu, Sikh or Buddhist religious communities. The term 'Dalit' has fewer problems than alternatives like 'SC', 'ex-untouchable', 'Harijan' and so on' (Deshpande, 2009, p. 13).

12 (Trivedi et al., 2016, pp. 33–34)

13 (Trivedi et al., 2016, p. 35)

14 For an excellent overview of this debate, see Nasreen Fazalbhoy, 2005.

15 For an elaborated discussion on this question see: deSouza et al, 2019, Chapter 4.

16 'BJP managed to convince people we are a Muslim party: Sonia Gandhi', *Indian Express*, https://indianexpress.com/article/india/bjp-managed-to-convince-people-we-are-a-muslim-party-sonia-gandhi-5092572/.

17 'Four Years of Modi Government - Economic and Social Transformation', 16 June 2018, https://www.kamalsandesh.org/four-years-modi-government-economic-social-transformation/0/, accessed on 9 August 2023.

18 'STATUS OF FOLLOW-UP ACTION ON THE DECISIONS OF GOVERNMENT ON SACHAR

COMMITTEE RECOMMENDATIONS (As on 31.03.2019)', https://www.minorityaffairs.gov.in/ WriteReadData/RTF1984/2286191517.pdf.

19 Reports | Ministry of Minority Affairs | Government of India, https://minorityaffairs.gov.in/show_content. php?lang=1&level=1&ls_id=339&lid=273

20 https://www.minorityaffairs.gov.in/sites/default/files/ EVALUATION OF PM%27s 15 PP.pdf

21 'Politics Between Elections', https://www.lokniti.org/ PoliticsandSocietybetweenElections, accessed on 9 August 2023

22 Ahmed, 2019 c.

23 Khalid Ansari makes a persuasive argument in this regard. He questions the minority -majority framework from the vantage point of the Pasmanda discourse--the assertion of marginalized Muslims against the caste-based domination. Ansari suggests, 'the extant social and political conditions that circumscribe the democratic aspirations of Pasmanda Muslims have probably exceeded the context that legitimated the earlier imagination of the minority space, and therefore the ensemble of emerging contestations around recognition/ social justice, majority–minority and secular–communal duopolies, or reform may be provisionally termed as "post-minority". It does not necessarily mean the negation of earlier concerns around religious communalism or majority assimilationism that quintessentially defined the minority space, but rather an appreciation for the dynamic nature of social space and the democratic possibilities opened by recent normative/symbolic inversions inaugurated by subaltern movements' (Ansari, 2021, p.122).

24 B.R. Ambedkar, 1943, *Pakistan or the Partition of India*, http://www.columbia.edu/itc/mealac/pritchett/00ambedkar/ ambedkar_partition/, accessed on 9 August 2023.

25 I have devoted a chapter to explain the significance of Hindutva in the internal configuration of Muslim identity in my book Siyasi Muslims. (Ahmed, 2019, pp. 63–82)

26 The recent Youth Study is a good example. Total 33 Muslim respondents at the all-India level (around 3 per cent of the total Muslim responders) did not mention their caste.

Chapter 8: New India and the Muslim Political

1 This line of argument is not entirely new. The serious commentators of Indian democracy often invoke the crucial political presence of Muslims in India to measure the success of Indian democracy. One of the most noticeable explanations comes from Arend Lijphart, who describes Indian democracy as a consociational democracy. According to Lijphart, Indian case fulfil four basic features of consociational democracy: (1) grand coalition governments that include representatives of all major linguistic and religious groups, (2) cultural autonomy for these groups, (3) proportionality in political representation and civil service appointments, and (4) a minority veto with regard to vital minority rights and autonomy. He argues that 'newly independent India embraced power sharing and has maintained it ever since is not even very surprising . . . After the late 1960s, as a result of greater mass mobilization and activation, power sharing became less strong and pervasive, evidenced by the centralization of the Congress Party and the federal system, the decline of the Congress Party's electoral strength, the attack on minority rights, and the rise of the BJP. As consociational theory would have predicted, Indian democracy has remained basically stable, but the weakening of power sharing has been accompanied by an increase in intergroup hostility and violence. Concern about these trends is reflected in the consociational thrust

of the major proposals for political and constitutional change by reform-minded Indians' (Lijphart, 1996, p. 266). Interestingly, Muslim political participation is seen as a given and uncomplicated element in this analytical framework. It appears that Lijphart does not look at the discursive making of Muslim identities and their political manifestations. Steven Wilkinson's critique of consociational explanation is also very relevant here. Wilkinson argues that identities are not always fixed and therefore, power sharing needs to be examined in relation to changing dynamics of electoral competition (Wilkinson, 2004, pp. 134–136).

2   Ahmed, 2016, pp. 348–374.
3   For an excellent critique of the *celebrationist* view of Indian democracy, see, Das, 2015, pp. 1–28.
4   Mohan Bhagwat's comment that Hindutva without Muslims is meaningless is very relevant here. See Ahmed, 2019.
5   There are certainly a few very detailed studies on the Muslim political participation in the 1970s and 1980s. The CSDS-Lokniti has been collecting data on Muslim electoral behavior regularly since 1996. This valuable literature, however, has not been studied systematically.
6   Lawrence A. Scaff introduces us to these two concepts of political participation. Scaff argues that participation as interaction should not be juxtaposed with participation as an instrumental action (Scaff, 1975, pp. 442–462). I find this argument very valuable because it helps us in unpacking the ways in which the idea of *Muslim political action* is formed in public debates, especially in post-2014 period.
7   The methodology adopted by the Sachar Commission Report is a good example of this view of political participation. The Report notes: 'It is useful to distinguish between three types of overlapping issues . . . faced by the Muslim community in India: *Issues that are common to all poor*

people (Muslims are largely poor), *Issues that are common to all minorities, Issues that are specific to Muslims*. For example, several concerns relating to employment and education specific to Muslims may fall in the first category. Similarly, some aspects of identity and security may be common across minorities while some others may be specific to Muslims'. (Emphasis added, PMHLC, 2006, p. 4)

8   I draw heavily on Mukulika Banerjee's work on everyday politics of Indian elections to make this point. Responding to the question, *'why do people vote?'* she introduces us to the complex web of relationship which determine political choices at various level. See, Banerjee, 2014.

9   It is important to clarify here that this form of political action cannot be reduced to the popular notion of *Muslim vote bank*. The imagination that Muslims do have certain collective interests, which eventually determine their political actions, is highly misleading. Muslims certainly bargain with the state as a group; but these political transactions, as this paper tries to demonstrate, always remain highly diversified. These diversified Muslim responses must be seen in relation to what Akhil Gupta calls the imagined state of everyday life. See, Gupta, 1995, pp. 375–402.

10 Ramachandran 2020.

11 For a detailed discussion on Muslims' reactions to aggressive Hindutva driven discourse of nationalism in the post-2014 period, see, Ahmed, 2019, Chapter 11.

12 The anti-CAA protesters, especially Muslims were systematically targeted by the state. It underlines the fact that the ruling party is keen to use Muslim assertiveness to strengthen and consolidate its Hindutva constituency. See 'Police chargesheet 15 for "conspiracy", link Delhi riots to anti-CAA protests', Mahender Singh Manral, *Indian Express*, 17 September 2020, https://indianexpress.com/

article/cities/delhi/police-chargesheet-15-for-conspiracy-link-delhi-riots-to-anti-caa-protests-6599046/ accessed on 23 September 2020.

13 Delhi's Shaheen Bagh—a protest site near the Jamia Millia Islamia University—acquired a powerful symbolic status and inspired many Muslims led protests against CAA/NRC in the country. However, Muslim reactions to CAA should not be reduced to the Shaheen Bagh phenomenon. For a detailed discussion on Shaheen Bagh protest, see Salam, 2020.

14 Rahul Rao describes this phenomenon as 'nationalism against the state'. See Rao, 2020.

15 'They Need No Saviours, They Are the Saviours: What the Resolute, Unafraid Presence of Muslim Women Tells Us', Ghazala Jamil, *Outlook*, 7 February 2020, https://www.outlookindia.com/magazine/story/india-news-opinion-hats-off-to-protesting-muslim-women-who-have-successfully-deflated-majoritarian-nationalism/302755, accessed on 19 May 2020.

16 'Lokniti-CSDS Survey: Social and Political Barometer 2023', https://www.lokniti.org/content/Lokniti-CSDS-Survey

17 National Election Study 2019, UP Assembly Election Study 2022.

18 '20% are those who oppose Ram Janmabhoomi, sympathise with terrorists: Yogi on "80 vs 20" remark', *India Today*, 10 January 2020, https://www.indiatoday.in/elections/uttar-pradesh-assembly-polls-2022/story/uttar-pradesh-cm-yogi-adityanath-80-20-a-reality-assembly-polls-panchayat-aaj-tak-votes-1898390-2022-01-10.

19 'UP election results: 36 Muslim MLAs elected—up from 24 in 2017 polls', Asad Rahman, *Indian Express*, 11 March 2022, https://indianexpress.com/elections/up-election-results-36-muslim-mlas-elected-7814463/

20 'Party-wise Trend and Results 2022', Election Commission of India (eci.gov.in), accessed on 17 October 2023.

In Lieu of a Conclusion

1   'Address by Shri Jagdeep Dhankhar, Honourable Vice President & Chairman Rajya Sabha at the Inauguration of the 83rd All India Conference of Presiding Officers' in Jaipur on January 11, 2023', https://vicepresidentofindia.nic.in/speechesinterviews/address-shri-jagdeep-dhankhar-honourable-vice-president-chairman-rajya-sabha

2   'Basic Structure doctrine guides judges like North Star, says CJI DY Chandrachud after Vice President Dhankhar calls doctrine incorrect', *Bar and Bench*, 22 January 2023, https://www.barandbench.com/news/basic-structure-doctrine-guides-judges-like-north-star-says-cji-dy-chandrachud-after-vice-president-dhankhar-calls-doctrine-incorrect.

3   Ibid.

4   'Haryana Violence: How Provocative Videos and a Background of Hate Preceded the Nuh Riots', Wire, https://thewire.in/communalism/haryana-violence-mewat-hate-and-provocative-videos

5   'Buildings Of Particular Community Brought Down As Exercise Of Ethnic Cleansing?': Punjab & Haryana High Court Asks On Nuh-Gurugram Demolitions', Aiman J. Chishti, Live Law, 7 August 2023, https://www.livelaw.in/top-stories/punjab-haryana-high-court-asks-on-nuh-demolition-drive-whether-buildings-belonging-to-particular-community-brought-down-as-exercise-of-ethnic-cleansing-234623

6   'Karnataka verdict: Congress attributes victory to "Bharat Jodo Yatra"', *Tribune India*, 13 May 2023, https://

www.tribuneindia.com/news/nation/karnataka-verdict-congress-attributes-victory-to-bharat-jodo-yatra-507529

7   'Bharat Jodo Yatra: Over 200 Civil Society Members Appeal People To Support Congress' Initiative', *Outlook*, 6 September 2022, https://www.outlookindia.com/national/-over-200-civil-society-members-appeal-people-to-support-congress-bharat-jodo-yatra--news-221328.

8   Kothari, 1984.

9   Partha Chatterjee, 2008.

10   'AAP changes party constitution, Kejriwal to continue as chief', Nikhil M. Babu, *The Hindu*, 29 January 2021, https://www.thehindu.com/news/cities/Delhi/aap-changes-party-constitution-kejriwal-to-continue-as-chief/article33688675.ece

11   Partha Chatterjee, 2019, p. 152.

12   Defending India's Swadharma-2019 & Beyond, https://www.youtube.com/watch?v=869qMCeh1tA& feature=youtu.be.

13   'Defending India's Swadhrama: 2019 and Beyond', https://puneinternationalcentre.org/event/defending-indias-swadharma-2019-beyond/, accessed on 17 October 2023.

14   'Modi said CAA protests anti-national, just like Indira Gandhi did before declaring Emergency, Yogendra Yadav', Print, 7 February 2020, https://theprint.in/opinion/modi-said-caa-protests-anti-national-just-like-indira-gandhi-did-before-declaring-emergency/361501/

15   Garm Hava - गरम हवा | HD Quality Indian Classic - Balraj Sahni | Farooq Shaikh | Kaifi Azmi | 1974, https://www.youtube.com/watch?v=eHfrHDBxCFU&ab_channel=TheCinemaArchives

Acknowledgements

I always find it hard to write a satisfactory 'acknowledgement' for two reasons. The first reason is inextricably linked to the nature of social science research. It is almost impossible to draw a clear dividing line between what has been borrowed from others and what is exactly the 'original contribution'. An individual researcher is a product of a society, which shapes his/her thinking, world view and futuristic imaginations. It does not, however, mean that the researcher is a static–machinal entity. S/he interprets the world, constructs a set of plausible narratives, engages with the messiness of the social order, and even tries to intervene in it, in a rather slow and gradual manner. It is not an easy task to explicate the nuances of this dialectical and organic relationship between a researcher and his/her social world. Therefore, the best feasible way to recognize the social nature of academic research is to honour those processes by which individual ideas are produced, organized, regulated and presented.

The second reason is more practical. Intellectual support comes from a variety of sources—institutions, networks, teachers, colleagues, reviewers, readers, students, research staff, respondents, friends and even those unknown individuals who make constructive comments in seminars and on social media. It is difficult to acknowledge the individual contribution of each person(s). I, therefore, express my gratitude to all my readers, colleagues and fellow travellers for their comments and criticisms.

This book would not have been possible without the institutional and intellectual support provided by the Centre for the Study of Developing Societies (CSDS)—popularly known as the 'Centre' in the world of Indian social sciences.

The work benefited immensely from conversations with my colleagues at CSDS. I am grateful to Ashis Nandy, Shail Mayaram, Rajeev Bhargava, Peter deSouza, Sanjeer Alam, Sanjay Kumar, Aditya Nigam, Abhay Kumar Dubey, Awadhendra Sharan, Prathama Banerjee, Priyadarshini Vijaisri, Rakesh Pandey, Ravi Sundaram, Ravi Vasudevan, Ravi Kant, Praveen Rai, Nishikant Kolge, Baidik Bhattacharya, Prabhat Kumar and Ananya Vajpeyi for their support and encouragement.

I am also grateful to the CSDS library and staff and my Lokniti friends—Himanshu, Prithi, Harsh, R. Natrajan, Ranjeet, Manoj, Ayodhya, Vicky, Dhanajay and others for their support, especially Manan Shivhare and Harsha Singh, who worked as research assistants for this project.

Intellectual discussions with Nilanjan Mukhopadhyay, Rama Lakshami, Nilanjana Kaviraj, S. Irfan Habib, Sanjay Pugalia, Rahul Verma, Ravish Kumar, Manoj Kumar Jha, Tani Bhargava, Khalid Anis Ansari, Christophe Jaffrelot, Milan Vaishnav, Mahesh Rangarajan, Uddalak Mukherjee, Riaz Ahmad, late Imitaz Ahmad, Shaikh Mujib-ur-Rehman, Manash Firaq Bhattacharjee, Hyder Khan, Ali Anwar Ansari, Varghese K. George, Gurpreet Mahajan, Ajay Gudavarthy, Satish Kumar Jha, Kamal Nayan Choubey, Dhananjay Rai, Amitabh Rai, Ather Farouqui, Yatindra Singh Sisodia, Ashutosh Kumar, Sanjay Lodha, Mohammad Sajjad, Neeti Nair, Amir Ullah Khan, Tanweer Fazal, Ghazala Wahab, Mithlesh Kumar Jha, Irfan Engineer, Syed Ubaidur Rehman, Zoya Hasan, M. Ghazali Khan, Ravi Sinha, Mary John, Satish Deshpande, Murat Akan, Pooja Pillai, Atul Chaurasia, Ashutosh Varshney, Rajeshwari Deshpande, Suhas Palshikar,

Sandeep Shastri, M.R. Shamshad, Shamsul Islam, Raj Kumar Bhatia, Mahesh Sharma, Mukulika Banerjee, Ajay Skaria, Prithvi Shobhi, Tariq Thachil, Nivedita Menon, Saubhik Chakrabarti, Ujjwal Kumar Singh, Anupama Roy, Subrata K. Mitra, Rekha Saxena, Subir Sinha, Manisha Priyam, Manisha Pande, Mehmood Mamdani, Pratap Bhanu Menta, Pankaj Sharma, Vibha Atri, Jyoti Mishra, Zakia Soman, Vivek Shukla, Indrajeet Kumar Jha, Shahid Siddiqui, Kumar Prashant, Iqbal Ahmad, Irfan Ahmed, Ira Bhaskar, Rahul Dev, Milan Vaishnav, Purushottam Agarwal, Shamsul Islam, and Manoranjan Mohanty have always been very helpful in shaping my arguments. I am thankful to them.

I do not have words to describe the contribution of Madhulika Banerjee to my intellectual and personal life. She has been a source of inspiration for me for over three decades—as a sister, as a friend, as a guide and, above all, as a teacher.

My *ustad* M.N. Thakur has a special status in my life. I still believe that he is one of the most original thinkers of politics I have ever met. Intellectual discussions with him always give me the confidence to assert that creative emancipation is desirable, possible and achievable.

Yogendra Yadav has been my mentor. I admire his analytical ability, his courage of conviction and the calmness of his pro-people, principle-based politics of justice and equality. His creative ideas have shaped many of the arguments presented in this book. I do not have adequate words to express my gratitude for him.

I lost my close friend and cousin Maulana Syed Athar Hussain Delhvai last year. He was a gifted Islamic scholar and thinker. He was my *peer*. My interpretation of Indian Islam relies heavily on his writings and speeches. I am also fortunate to have friends like Jinee Lokaneeta, Manish Jain, Ruma Dutt, Abhay Prasad Singh, Mohammad Nadim, and Syed Zahid Ali.

I am grateful for them. My friendship with Vikram Nayak is exceptional. He is an amazingly creative thinker, painter and film-maker. He always encourages me to do more creative work.

A few words about my *guru*, Sudipta Kaviraj. He is one of the best-thinking minds India has ever produced. His originality is incomparable; his creativity is commendable and his simplicity is adorable. Apart from many things, he taught me the significance of honest intellectual work. His emphasis on pure 'thinking' always encourages me to question my own formulations, arguments and claims. I still feel his presence around me whenever I read or write something new. Thank you, sir, for everything!

My children—Sarmad Ahmed, Maaz Ahmed and Raheel Ahmed—have transformed us in a significant way. Sarmad's artistic creativity is admirable; Maaz is honest and truthful; and Raheel is committed and organized. They love us, they fight with us and they criticize us. Their presence makes my life meaningful and worthy. I am certainly thankful for their comments and criticisms.

Finally, I would like to thank my life partner Nazima Parveen for her love, support and intellectual comradeship. I always admire her calmness, organization and originality. She has always been a source of inspiration for me. I have learnt a lot from her. The formulations and arguments presented in this book are the outcome of our endless discussions, especially the morning sessions, which she jokingly calls *chai pe charcha*. In this sense, she is the first reader, first critique, first reviewer and eventually an invisible co-author of this book! In recognition of all this, I dedicate this work to her.

My sincere thanks to Penguin Random House India for recognizing the significance of this subject. I am particularly thankful to Karthik Venkatesh and Premanka Goswami for their support and encouragement.

Scan QR code to access the
Penguin Random House India website